CALCULATORS
Printing & Display

William R. Pasewark
Professor Emeritus
Texas Tech University
Lubbock, Texas

Office Management Consultant

SOUTH-WESTERN
CENGAGE Learning

Australia • Brazil • Japan • Korea • Mexico • Singapore • Spain • United Kingdom • United States

SOUTH-WESTERN
CENGAGE Learning

Calculators: Printing & Display,
Fifth Edition
William R. Pasewark

Vice President of Editorial, Business: Jack W. Calhoun

Vice President/Editor-in-Chief: Karen Schmohe

Senior Developmental Editor: Penny Shank

Consulting Editor: Kathy Schaefer

Senior Marketing Communications Manager: Sarah Greber

Marketing Manager: Alla Reese

Content Project Management: PreMediaGlobal

Senior Manufacturing Coordinator: Charlene Taylor

Production Service: PreMediaGlobal

Senior Art Director: Tippy McIntosh

Internal Design: PreMediaGlobal

Cover Design: Lou Ann Thesing

Cover Image: ©Mike Flippo, Shutterstock

Photography Manager: Deanna Ettinger

Photo Researcher: Darren Wright

For product information and technology assistance, contact us at
Cengage Learning Customer & Sales Support, 1-800-354-9706

For permission to use material from this text or product,
submit all requests online at **www.cengage.com/permissions**
Further permissions questions can be emailed to
permissionrequest@cengage.com

Student Edition ISBN-13: 978-0-8400-6535-3

Student Edition ISBN-10: 0-8400-6535-3

South-Western Cengage Learning
5191 Natorp Boulevard
Mason, OH 45040
USA

Cengage Learning products are represented in Canada by Nelson Education, Ltd.

For your course and learning solutions, visit **school.cengage.com**

All images and art © Cengage Learning 2012

Printed in the United States of America
2 3 4 5 6 7 17 16 15 14

Contents

About the Author, Acknowledgements, and Reviewers

About the Author

William R. Pasewark, Sr., earned a PhD at New York University. He taught both Business and Education courses at NYU, Michigan State, Penn State, and Texas Tech. Bill authored 105 best-selling business and computer books, seven of which won Texty Awards from the Text and Academic Authors Association. Work experience includes: several jobs in the Wall Street section of NYC; Office Management Consultant; Marine Corps Sergeant in the Iwo Jima Invasion; General Manager of Pasewark LTD, a textbook authoring family partnership. Bill has lectured in 31 states and several foreign countries. He attended 60 continuous NBEA conventions and was a registered lobbyist to require Business courses in high schools.

Acknowledgements

The author thanks Su Pasewark Hess and Kathy Schaefer for their dedicated and effective work on *Calculators: Printing & Display*.

Many professional South-Western sales representatives make educationally sound presentations to teachers. The author knows of and appreciates very much a sales representative's valuable function as a "bridge" between the author and teachers.

Reviewers

Special appreciation is extended to the following teachers who provided valuable feedback by responding to our surveys.

Alice Matthews
Charlestown High School
Charlestown, IN

Alice McDonough
Montana Technical
Butte, MT

Barbara Allender
Capital Area Career Center
Mason, MI

Brian Wilson
College of Marin
Kentfield, CA

Deb Bixby
North Carroll High School
Hampstead, MD

Dorothy Dean
Illinois Central College
East Peoria, IL

Dot Butler
Tennessee Technical Center
Crump, TN

Marilou Grimes
Eastside High School
Covington, GA

Jill Fisher
Indian Capital Tech
Tahlequah, OK

Kathleen Holliman
Wallace State Community College
Selma, AL

Kimberly Rogers
Ashland High School
Ashland, OH

Doreen Kruger
Tri-County Area School District
Plainfield, WI

Carol Lehrer
Santa Ana College
Santa Ana, CA

Linda Estrada
Bakersfield Adult School
Bakersfield, CA

Mary Ann Whitehurst
Southern Crescent Technical College
Griffin, GA

Michelle Hedberg
Wayne County Schools Career
 Center
Smithville, OH

Nita Kinney
McLoughlin High School
Milton-Freewater, OR

Sharon Green
Three Rivers Community College
Poplar Bluff, MO

Achievable Learning Objectives

This text-workbook was developed around fundamental learning objectives that are important in students' personal and business lives and include:

1. developing workplace competence using the ten-key numeric touch method.
2. solving common business and personal math problems using a calculator.
3. understanding the value and importance of calculators in business.
4. improving basic arithmetic skills.

Instructional Package

The complete instructional package includes:

1. A text-workbook (ISBN: 0-8400-6535-3) containing 30 jobs based on current business procedures with the following features:
   a. Twenty jobs to help students learn the touch method and solve business and personal math problems on a calculator.
   b. Ten simulation jobs relating to earnings, banking services, credit use, stock transactions, household expenditures, automobile finances, insurance, and school-related math problems.
   c. Two production drills in which students calculate auto repair orders.
   d. A Student Data Sheet that will acquaint teachers with students and provide practice for students in completing employment applications.
   e. Applications for Your Life that show the immediate use of calculator applications to your life.
   f. Arrow icons in the first ten jobs that signal when you will operate the calculator.
   g. Instructions on the systematic methods of correcting errors and proving and verifying answers.
   h. Handwritten numbers to give students practice in working with documents in business that are completed by hand.
   i. Reinforcement of legible number writing.
   j. Numerical proofreading exercises.
   k. Explanation of special function keys on calculators such as Constant Keys, Memory Keys, and Decimal Selectors.
   l. An Appendix that contains Reference Resources, Drills and Progress Records, Tables, Support Materials, and an Index.
2. A Test Packet (ISBN: 0-8400-6575-2) available to adopters of CALCULATORS that includes a Diagnostic Arithmetic Pretest and seven Progress Tests. Students record their test scores on the Progress Test Record on page 113 of the Appendix.
3. A Test Packet Key (ISBN: 0-8400-6576-0) available at no charge to adopters of CALCULATORS.
4. An Annotated Instructor's Edition (ISBN: 0-8400-6574-4) available at no charge to adopters of CALCULATORS that includes suggestions for planning and teaching the course and answers to all problems in the text-workbook.

Variety of Instructional Plans

CALCULATORS is a flexible text-workbook that can be effectively used in many different instructional plans including rotation, battery, individualized, cooperative, simulated office, or in short courses where office machines are taught.

Instructional Learning Features

The instructional design for CALCULATORS is based on modern instructional methods and the philosophy that learning should be meaningful, challenging, and enjoyable. The wide variety of hands-on, business-oriented activities will help motivate students to achieve the goals for the course. Some of the learning features include:

1. A Diagnostic Arithmetic Pretest that will help to determine the students' math abilities.
2. Step-by-step instructions on the touch method that include illustrations of important operation techniques.
3. Easy-to-read, self-instructional text.
4. Illustrations and explanations for each reach to a newly introduced key for both right- and left-handed operation.
5. Warm-Up Drills, Speed Drills, Accuracy Drills, and Technique Drills to help students improve their ten-key touch method proficiency.
6. Ten-Key Numeric Drills and Tests to help students improve speed and accuracy.
7. Progress Records to help students track their ten-key touch method progress.
8. Basic arithmetic practice, including estimating answers, proving answers, and working with fractions, decimals, and percents.
9. A wide variety of more than 1,100 problems that give students practice in a "simple-to-complex" pattern of learning.
10. Photos that show good working habits and proper calculator operation.
11. "Connectors" that are used when students are learning the touch method. This means that the last digit in an addend (456) is also the first digit in the next addend (645).
12. Seven Progress Tests to determine the students' skills at the end of every fifth job and at the end of the course.

Functional Format

The carefully designed format of the book helps make the numeric touch method learnable.

1. Enumerated instructions make it easy for students to read the text then operate the calculator in a step-by-step sequence.
2. A spiral binding enables students to handle the book easily.
3. The problems and answers are detachable so that the instructional material remains in the book for use in future jobs.

Realistic Grading System

A grading system has been devised based on the abilities of the students and the types of calculators in your course.

1. A Drills and Progress Records section in the Appendix enables students to record their test scores and chart their progress.
2. Answer columns are placed at the right edge of each page so several pages can be "fanned out" and scored simultaneously.
3. A Diagnostic Arithmetic Pretest and seven Progress Tests are available in a separate packet.
4. Rules for rounding decimals are given in the Appendix so that when followed, the students' answers will match those in the Instructor's Edition.

Ten-Key Numeric Touch Method

The ten-key numeric touch method means striking the numbered keys (0 through 9) and some function keys (such as the Add Key and Total Key) on the calculator *without looking at the keypad*. The ten-key numeric touch method is the universal means of entering numeric data into a wide variety of office machines such as calculators and the numeric keypad of computers.

Students must learn and use only the ten-key numeric touch method from the beginning, rather than looking at the keypad and striking all keys with the same finger. With proper practice, the touch method is faster, more accurate, and uses less head and hand movement in comparison with "hunting and pecking."

Ten-Key Numeric Test

The ten-key numeric keypad has become the universal keypad for high-speed, accurate inputting of numbers. Efficient inputting of numeric data on a wide variety of electronic keypads, such as calculators, computers, bank proofing machines, and cash registers, has become important in business to increase office productivity. To measure and compare productivity, it was necessary to create a standardized measuring instrument—the Ten-Key Numeric Test.

This test, located on pages 131 and 133, was developed for a research project called *Measuring Productivity on the Ten-Key Numeric Keypad Using Strokes a Minute and Errors a Minute*, by William R. Pasewark, hereafter referred to as the TKNStudy. Findings from the TKNStudy are used extensively in this book.

The Instructor's Manual includes standards (see page IM-7) based on scores from 18 high schools in 5 states. The standards are based on Strokes a Minute (SAM) and Errors a Minute (EAM) similar to those used for keyboarding timed writing tests in schools and for applicants seeking employment in businesses. There is a need to standardize measurement on the ten-key numeric keypad so that teaching methodology can be improved to increase productivity. This study will be continued and new data will be added to the compilation of scores. This will keep the national standards current with improvements made in calculators and learning methodology.

The TKNStudy was the first field-tested research to measure and thereby improve productivity on the ten-key numeric keypad.

In conjunction with the TKNStudy, drills were developed to improve SAM and EAM productivity. Drills were also prepared to improve technique, speed, and accuracy. These drills are located on pages 112, 114, 115, and 117.

The Ten-Key Numeric Calculator Proficiency Certificate on page 129 can be used to record the student's best SAM and EAM. Students can present the certificate to prospective employers.

Additional Ten-Key Touch Method Instruction

To further develop competencies on calculators, you may want to consider the following publications:

1. TEN-KEY SKILL BUILDER FOR CALCULATORS, 2E, ISBN: 0-538-69274-X, South-Western Cengage Learning. A concise book designed for intensive skill building of speed and accuracy on the ten-key calculator. Completion time: 10 to 15 hours.
2. CALCULATOR SIMULATION, 5E, ISBN: 0-538-68946-3, South-Western Cengage Learning. A calculator simulation in which students complete jobs for seven realistic companies using a variety of business forms. Completion time: 30 to 40 hours.
3. CALCULATOR SIMULATION, 5E, SHORT COURSE, ISBN: 0-538-68948-X, South-Western Cengage Learning. A calculator simulation for shortened or block courses in which students complete jobs for four realistic companies using a variety of business forms. Completion time: 10 to 20 hours.

Introduction

Goal of This Book

The goal of CALCULATORS: PRINTING & DISPLAY is to help you develop a touch-method mastery on the ten-key calculator. After completing this book, you will be able to use any desktop calculator to solve common business and personal math problems. The ten-key numeric touch method can also be used on other business machines such as the numeric keypads of computers, bank proofing machines, and cash registers.

The Ten-Key Touch Method

Calculators are fast, accurate, and easy to use when operated properly. Therefore, it is important to learn and use only the ten-key touch method from the beginning, rather than looking at the keypad and striking all keys with the same finger. With proper practice, the touch method is faster, more accurate, and uses less head and hand movement in comparison with "hunting and pecking."

Benefits for You

Calculators are used in many modern offices. To be successful on the job, learn how to operate the calculator efficiently. You will be able to apply what you learn in this book because many of the problems are based on calculations done in the business world such as stock transactions, casualty insurance, and auto repair orders. Problems also involve calculations done in personal life such as checking accounts, budgets, and the cost of using credit.

Your Learning Objectives

The objectives of this book are to help you:
1. develop competence using the ten-key numeric touch method.
2. solve common business and personal math problems using a calculator.
3. understand the value and importance of calculators in business.
4. improve your basic arithmetic skills.

Learning Features

This book was written to make your learning as easy, effective, and enjoyable as possible. The learning features include:
1. short, clear instructions with illustrations showing how to master the touch method.
2. a variety of activities that will keep you interested in learning calculator operation and arithmetic.
3. learning objectives stated at the beginning of each job so you will know exactly what you should accomplish.
4. arrow icons in the first ten jobs that signal when you will operate the calculator.
5. a "simple-to-complex" pattern of learning to make it easy for you to progress according to your abilities.
6. answers for the first problem of each new exercise so you will know after working the first problem if you understand how to solve that type of problem.
7. Applications for Your Life that show the immediate use of calculator applications to your life.
8. a variety of Warm-Up Drills, Speed Drills, Accuracy Drills, and Technique Drills that will give you a chance to improve each time you work a drill.
9. a unique method of measuring speed and accuracy using Strokes a Minute (SAM) and Errors a Minute (EAM) similar to keyboarding scores.
10. SAM and EAM Graphs that enable you to record your scores from drills and chart your progress throughout the course.
11. two Production Drills that will give you realistic experience in handling business forms.
12. a Diagnostic Arithmetic Pretest that will help you determine the math areas in which you may need improvement.
13. a review of basic arithmetic including fractions, percents, and decimals.
14. a Ten-Key Proficiency Certificate upon completion of the course that you can present to a prospective employer.

Illus. I-1
The touch method can be used on a variety of business machines that have ten-key numeric keypads.

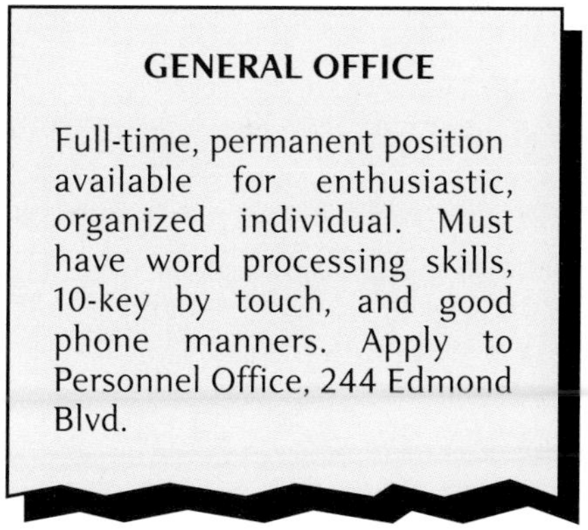

GENERAL OFFICE

Full-time, permanent position available for enthusiastic, organized individual. Must have word processing skills, 10-key by touch, and good phone manners. Apply to Personnel Office, 244 Edmond Blvd.

Illus. I-2
There are many jobs available for people with the office skills you will learn from this book.

Calculator Parts

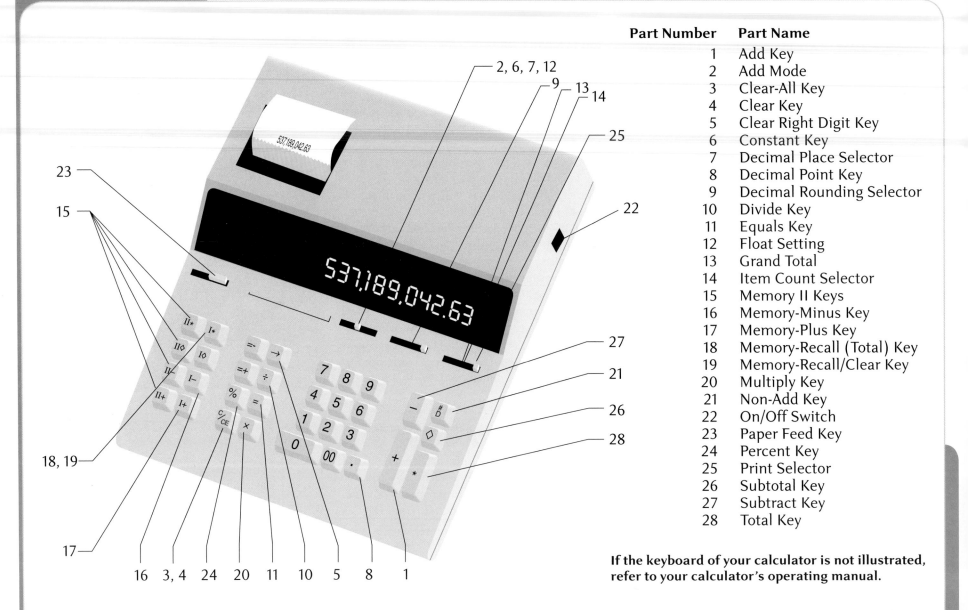

Part Number	Part Name
1	Add Key
2	Add Mode
3	Clear-All Key
4	Clear Key
5	Clear Right Digit Key
6	Constant Key
7	Decimal Place Selector
8	Decimal Point Key
9	Decimal Rounding Selector
10	Divide Key
11	Equals Key
12	Float Setting
13	Grand Total
14	Item Count Selector
15	Memory II Keys
16	Memory-Minus Key
17	Memory-Plus Key
18	Memory-Recall (Total) Key
19	Memory-Recall/Clear Key
20	Multiply Key
21	Non-Add Key
22	On/Off Switch
23	Paper Feed Key
24	Percent Key
25	Print Selector
26	Subtotal Key
27	Subtract Key
28	Total Key

If the keyboard of your calculator is not illustrated, refer to your calculator's operating manual.

Job 1
Addition; Touch Method: 4, 5, 6 Keys

NAME_____ DATE_____ PERIOD_____ GRADE_____

LEARNING OBJECTIVES

1. Use the touch method to enter the digits 4, 5, and 6.
2. Solve addition problems.

GETTING READY

1. Connect your calculator to an electrical outlet.
2. Clear your desk of everything except your calculator, book, and pencil or pen.
3. Place your book and calculator so you can easily read the book and operate the calculator. You may operate the calculator with either your left hand or right hand.
4. Turn your calculator on with the On/Off Switch `22`.
5. **Function keys** control the operation of the calculator. You must anticipate the functions needed to solve each group of problems. Set the following function keys:
   a. Decimal Place Selector `7`* at *0.*
   b. Item Count Selector `14` at *Off.*
   c. Print Selector `25` at *On.*
6. Strike the Clear-All Key `3`. A **clear symbol** such as *0, 0A, 0C,* or *0.CA* should print on the tape. (On some calculators, it may be necessary to strike another key.)
7. Sit in a comfortable position with your:
   a. Eyes on the copy.
   b. Fingers on the home-row keys (4, 5, and 6).
   c. Back straight.
   d. Feet flat on the floor.

Use these *Getting Ready* procedures at the beginning of all future jobs.

*Throughout this book, use the boxed numbers ☐ to locate calculator parts in the illustration on page 2.

Position your book and calculator at a comfortable angle.

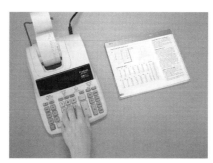

Illus. 1-A
Left-Hand Operation.

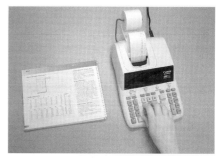

Illus. 1-B
Right-Hand Operation.

Eyes on copy

Fingers on home-row keys

Back straight

Feet flat on floor

Illus. 1-C
Practice correct posture.

Using the Touch Method

Keep your hand correctly positioned on the home-row keys—4, 5, and 6.

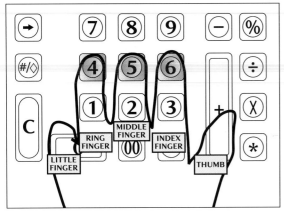

Illus. 1-D
Left-Hand Operation.

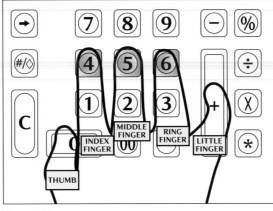

Illus. 1-E
Right-Hand Operation.

	Left-Hand Operation	Right-Hand Operation
Index Finger	6	4
Middle Finger	5	5
Ring Finger	4	6
Little Finger	0	Add Key, Total Key
Thumb	Add Key, Total Key	0

Illus. 1-F
Use the correct finger placement for the touch method.

USING THE TOUCH METHOD

The **ten-key numeric touch method** means striking the numbered keys and some function keys—*without looking at the keypad*. The keys are located by "touch" when you keep the index, middle, and ring fingers over the 4, 5, and 6 Keys. These are the **home-row keys**.

It is easier to strike keys with your writing hand instead of your nonwriting hand. However, you may prefer to develop the ten-key numeric touch method using your nonwriting hand, leaving your writing hand free to write answers and turn pages in this book.

The home-row keys may be more hollow than the other keys, and the 5 Key may have a raised dot to help you find the home row by touch. Keep your wrist straight and your fingers curved over the home-row keys. *As you learn to use the home-row keys by touch, emphasize accuracy rather than speed.*

Use the touch method to complete each step on page 5 as you read it. The chart at the left will help you determine which finger to use when striking the home-row keys, Add Key, and Total Key.

Illus. 1-G
Curve your fingers over the home-row keys.

NAME_____ DATE_____ PERIOD_____ GRADE_____

➤ USING THE TOUCH METHOD (continued)*

1. LOOK AT THE KEYPAD and use the correct finger to strike the 4 Key three times. Strike the 4 Key with the ring finger if you use your left hand or with the index finger if you use your right hand.
2. Strike the Add Key ⬚1. The Add Key is struck with the thumb if you use your left hand or with the little finger if you use your right hand. The number 444 will print on the calculator tape.
3. DO NOT LOOK AT THE KEYPAD and strike the 4 Key three more times. (If you make a mistake, clear the calculator by striking the Clear-All Key and start the problem again.)
4. Strike the Add Key.
5. Strike the Total Key ⬚28 to get your answer (888). The Total Key is struck with the thumb if you use your left hand or with the little finger if you use your right hand. Striking the Total Key will also clear the calculator for the next problem.
6. Repeat Steps 1–5 for the 5 Key and for the 6 Key. Strike the 5 Key with the middle finger of either hand. Strike the 6 Key with the index finger if you use your left hand or with the ring finger if you use your right hand.

➤ ADDITION

Always enter digits (the figures from 0 to 9) in the same order that you would write them—from left to right. When you are instructed to enter a number or strike a key, *tap* each key with a sharp, quick stroke.

The chart entitled **Steps for Adding** describes how to work the problem, *4 + 5 + 6*. The first column tells you what to do; the second column shows what will print on the tape; the third column shows what will appear in the window display. Each number to be added is called an **addend**. Now, complete the problem, *4 + 5 + 6*, using the touch method.

*Each time an arrow appears in Jobs 1–10, you will operate the calculator.

Using the Touch Method (continued)

Illus. 1-H
Your tape should look similar to this tape after you complete Step 6.

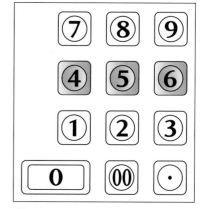

Illus. 1-I
Home-Row Keys.

Addition

Steps for Adding

Operation	Tape*	Display*
1. Clear the calculator.	0.CA	0
2. Enter the first addend (4).		4
3. Strike the Add Key.	4.+	4
4. Enter the next addend (5).		5
5. Strike the Add Key.	5.+	9
6. Enter the next addend (6).		6
7. Strike the Add Key.	6.+	15
8. Strike the Total Key.	15.*	15

*Symbols may differ on your calculator.

Touch Method–Problem 1

1.

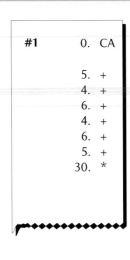

	5	
	4	
	6	
	4	
	6	
	5	
	30	

Illus. 1-J
Sample Tape for Problem 1.

```
#1      0.  CA

        5.  +
        4.  +
        6.  +
        4.  +
        6.  +
        5.  +
       30.  *
```

Home-Row Keys

2.	**3.**	**4.**	**5.**	**6.**	**7.**	**8.**
4	66	54	54	55	46	54
5	56	45	56	54	44	46
6	46	66	46	46	64	66
44	45	56	45	66	54	45
55	64	55	66	64	46	55
66	54	64	55	45	56	65

9.	**10.**	**11.**	**12.**	**13.**	**14.**	**15.**
44	44	444	654	666	544	545
55	56	555	555	556	454	464
46	54	666	456	664	564	655
64	55	466	446	456	466	546
54	64	446	545	654	544	465
65	46	665	454	464	654	565

Answers

1. _____ 30
2. _____
3. _____
4. _____
5. _____
6. _____
7. _____
8. _____
9. _____
10. _____
11. _____
12. _____
13. _____
14. _____
15. _____

➤ **TOUCH METHOD–PROBLEM 1**

Be sure the calculator is clear before starting each problem. Concentrate on using the touch method to strike each key sharply, quickly, and with the proper finger as you work Problem 1.

When the answer is provided, work each problem until your answer matches the book's answer. (See Illus. 1-J, the Sample Tape for Problem 1.)

➤ **HOME-ROW KEYS**

Complete Problem 2 by touch. When the answer is not in the book, write the answer with pen or pencil in the blank space below the problem.

Work the problem a second time.

1. If the second answer is the *same* as the first answer, you can assume that the answer is correct. Write the correct answer in the Answers column.

2. If the second answer is *different* from the first, write it below the first answer and repeat the problem until you get two answers that match. Then write the correct answer in the Answers column.

Tear the tape off when it is about as long as this page. Advance the tape before tearing it off by striking the Paper Feed Key [23]. Write each problem number on the tape, opposite the clear symbol. (See Illus. 1-J, the Sample Tape for Problem 1.)

Follow these procedures to solve Problems 3–15 and for all future calculating jobs.

COMPLETING THE JOB

After you finish all of the problems in a job:

1. If you have time, do the job again.
2. Provide the information where requested at the top of the page.
3. Remove each page at the perforation.
4. Attach the tapes behind the upper left corner of the pages.
5. Submit all your work as instructed by your teacher.
6. Turn your calculator off and cover it.

Job 2
Addition; Touch Method: 1, 2, 3, 7, 8, 9, 0, and 00 Keys

NAME_____ DATE_____ PERIOD_____ GRADE_____

LEARNING OBJECTIVES

1. Use the touch method to enter the digits 1, 2, 3, 7, 8, 9, 0, and 00.
2. Solve addition problems.

GETTING READY

Follow the instructions in Job 1, page 3, *Getting Ready*, to prepare for Job 2 and all future jobs.

➤ 7 KEY

1. Place your fingers on the home-row keys: 4, 5, and 6.
2. LOOK AT THE KEYPAD and form a picture in your mind of the reach up to the 7 Key. The 7 Key is struck with the ring finger if you use your left hand or with the index finger if you use your right hand. Practice reaching up to the 7 Key three times *without* actually entering the number.
3. WITHOUT LOOKING AT THE KEYS and keeping your fingers over the home-row keys, work Problems 1–3.

➤ 1 KEY

1. LOOK AT THE KEYPAD and form a picture in your mind of the reach down to the 1 Key. The 1 Key is struck with the ring finger if you use your left hand or with the index finger if you use your right hand. Practice reaching down to the 1 Key three times *without* actually entering the number.
2. WITHOUT LOOKING AT THE KEYS, work Problems 4–6.

Reach up from the 4 Key to strike the 7 Key.

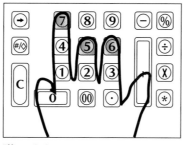

Illus. 2-A
Left-Hand Operation.

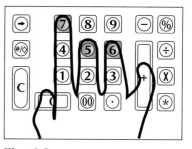

Illus. 2-B
Right-Hand Operation.

Reach down from the 4 Key to strike the 1 Key.

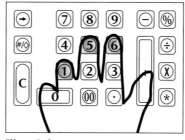

Illus. 2-C
Left-Hand Operation.

Illus. 2-D
Right-Hand Operation.

7 Key   1 Key

1.	2.	3.	4.	5.	6.	Answers
477	745	7	411	145	1	**1.** 3,212
777	567	75	111	561	14	**2.**
744	746	577	144	146	411	**3.**
457	674	764	451	611	156	**4.**
757	467	47	156	461	61	**5.**
3,212						**6.**

7

1, 4, and 7 Keys

7.	8.	9.	10.	11.	Answers
144	444	417	711	165	7. _____
714	517	764	451	57	8. _____
441	747	145	14	746	9. _____
174	166	444	477	641	10. _____
474	471	174	717	17	11. _____
					12. ____3,751____
					13. _____
					14. _____
					15. _____
					16. _____
					17. _____
					18. _____
					19. _____
					20. _____

Reach up from the 5 Key to strike the 8 Key.

Illus. 2-E
Left-Hand Operation.

Illus. 2-F
Right-Hand Operation.

➤ 1, 4, AND 7 KEYS
Without looking at the keypad, work Problems 7–11. Repeat the problems until it is easy for you to strike the keys at your fastest rate of speed.

8 Key / 2 Key / 00 Key

	8 Key			2 Key			00 Key	
Reach up from the 5 Key.			**Reach down from the 5 Key.**			**Reach down from the 5 Key.**		
12.	**13.**	**14.**	**15.**	**16.**	**17.**	**18.**	**19.**	**20.**
588	845	8	522	245	2	400	200	400
886	568	84	222	562	25	5,006	5,004	4,005
855	846	648	255	246	542	600	400	500
568	684	858	542	624	262	4,005	6,006	5,005
854	458	86	254	462	24	500	500	600
3,751								

➤ 8, 2, AND 00 KEYS
Strike the 8, 2, and 00 Keys with the middle finger of either hand. Problems 12–20 will help you develop stroking patterns so that when you see the numbers *8, 2,* and *00,* you will automatically strike these keys with your middle finger. Practice: 8, 2, and 00 Keys.

NAME_____ DATE_____ PERIOD_____ GRADE_____

➤ 2, 5, 8, AND 00 KEYS

Do not look at the keys as you work Problems 21–25. Repeat the problems until it is easy for you to strike the keys at your fastest rate of speed.

2, 5, 8, and 00 Keys

21.	22.	23.	24.	25.
225	2,008	1,258	552	81
858	825	84	2,004	200
500	528	572	85	5,005
285	800	6,008	800	42
800	58	26	5,672	785

Answers

21.	
22.	
23.	
24.	
25.	
26.	4,279
27.	
28.	
29.	
30.	
31.	
32.	
33.	
34.	

Reach up from the 6 Key to strike the 9 Key.

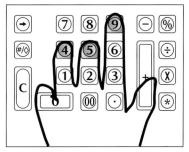

Illus. 2-G
Left-Hand Operation.

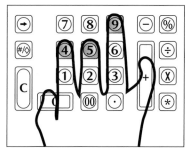

Illus. 2-H
Right-Hand Operation.

➤ 9 AND 3 KEYS

Strike the 9 and 3 Keys with the index finger if you use your left hand or with the ring finger if you use your right hand. Work Problems 26–31 in the usual manner.

➤ 3, 6, AND 9 KEYS

Do not look at the keys as you work Problems 32–34. Repeat the problems until it is easy for you to strike the keys at your fastest rate of speed.

9 Key			3 Key			3, 6, and 9 Keys		
Reach up from the 6 Key.			**Reach down from the 6 Key.**			**Return to the 6 Key.**		
26.	**27.**	**28.**	**29.**	**30.**	**31.**	**32.**	**33.**	**34.**
699	945	9	633	345	3	963	393	63
999	569	94	333	563	35	693	643	956
966	946	649	366	346	543	369	539	354
659	694	959	653	634	353	636	536	39
956	459	96	354	453	36	993	964	663
4,279								

0 Key

35.
```
  501
  106
  607
  701
  101
2,016
```

36.
```
 40
 10
405
170
 60
```

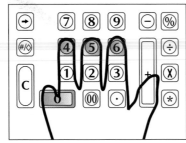

Strike the 0 (Zero) Key with your little finger.

Illus. 2-I
Left-Hand Operation.

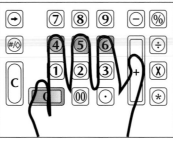

Strike the 0 (Zero) Key with your thumb.

Illus. 2-J
Right-Hand Operation.

All Numeric Keys

37.
```
484
562
390
117
800
```

38.
```
218
347
954
701
422
```

39.
```
739
963
147
503
291
```

40.
```
708
327
674
239
660
```

41.
```
365
781
168
457
953
```

42.
```
   48
2,003
  576
  811
   62
3,450
   17
  698
```

43.
```
 9,984
   671
 4,926
20,010
   645
 2,037
    89
   147
```

44.
```
 5,632
60,017
   480
    95
 3,467
70,036
   211
    54
```

45.
```
30,341
 3,244
   586
   193
793,511
 7,759
   502
17,580
```

46.
```
27,022
26,100
812,433
   489
21,883
   756
 1,131
 6,172
```

Answers

35.	2,016
36.	
37.	
38.	
39.	
40.	
41.	
42.	
43.	
44.	
45.	
46.	

➤ 0 KEY

Strike the 0 (Zero) Key with the little finger if you use your left hand or with the thumb if you use your right hand. Work Problems 35 and 36.

➤ ALL NUMERIC KEYS

Before beginning Job 3, you should be using the touch method to enter all numbers. Problems 37–46 will help you use the touch method to locate keys. Repeat the problems until it is easy for you to strike the keys at your fastest rate of speed.

COMPLETING THE JOB

After you finish all of the problems in a job:
1. If you have time, do the job again.
2. Provide the information where requested at the top of the page.
3. Remove each page at the perforation.
4. Attach the tapes behind the upper left corner of the pages.
5. Submit all your work as instructed by your teacher.
6. Turn your calculator off and cover it.
   Follow this procedure for all calculating jobs.

Job 3
Ten-Key Numeric Drill

NAME_____ DATE_____ PERIOD_____ GRADE_____

LEARNING OBJECTIVES

1. Complete a Ten-Key Numeric Drill (TKNDrill).
2. Calculate Strokes a Minute (SAM) and Errors a Minute (EAM).

TECHNIQUE CHECKLIST

As you complete Job 3, think about how you can improve your techniques to either increase speed or decrease errors. A Technique Checklist for the Ten-Key Numeric Touch Method is on page 116. Following the instructions at the top of the checklist, complete the checklist now to rate your present techniques.

➤ WARM-UP DRILL: 4, 5, AND 6 KEYS

The Warm-Up Drills at the beginning of each job have been included so that you will practice a variety of number combinations. These drills will help you to move your fingers with rhythm from one key to another using the touch method. Work each problem until each answer matches the book's answer.

Illus. 3-B
Ten-Key Keypad.

Illus. 3-A
Keep your eyes on the copy.

Warm-Up Drill: 4, 5, and 6 Keys

Strike each key with a rhythmic, bouncy touch.

545	564	546	644	665
556	456	625	586	548
654	565	574	149	693
456	564	204	403	705
564	456	598	254	612
646	656	461	761	564
3,421	3,261	3,008	2,797	3,787

Numbers With Many Digits

Bank Routing Numbers

1. 461 781 236
2. 118 153 132
3. 313 127 080

4. 667 519 436
5. 358 917 744
6. 463 123 516

Driver's License Numbers

7. 20-936-471
8. 03-593-678
9. 99-974-060

10. 28-831-034
11. 71-033-636
12. 97-577-999

Illus. 3-C
Keep your fingers curved over the home-row keys.

➤ NUMBERS WITH MANY DIGITS

You will see numbers with many digits in business. Touch enter the bank routing numbers and driver's license numbers in Problems 1–12. Spaces and hyphens will not appear in the display.

COMPLETING TEN-KEY NUMERIC DRILL #1

Read all instructions below before starting the drill on page 13.

Each problem in Ten-Key Numeric Drill #1 has 50 strokes.

A stroke occurs when any numerical key (0 through 9) or function key (such as the Add Key or Total Key) is entered into the calculator by striking that key. For example, in the first number, *9,067*, there are 5 strokes: 4 strokes for the digits *9067* and 1 stroke for the Add Key.

Each problem has 50 strokes because you will strike 41 digits, the Add Key 8 times, and the Total Key once.

NAME_____ DATE_____ PERIOD_____ GRADE_____

➤ TEN-KEY NUMERIC DRILL #1, ATTEMPT #1

To complete the drill, do the following:

1. Set the Print Selector at *On*.
2. Set the Decimal Place Selector at *0*.
3. Complete as many problems as you can in three minutes.
4. If you make an error while working a problem, disregard it and continue entering numbers.
5. Do not compare the answers on the tape to the answers below the problems until you complete the 3-minute timing.
6. Repeat the drill if you finish all 15 problems (A to O) before the end of three minutes.
7. Stop immediately at the end of the timing, even if you are in the middle of a number or a problem.

TEN-KEY NUMERIC DRILL #1

Each time you start a drill, concentrate on improving *either speed or accuracy*. Do not try to increase Strokes a Minute (SAM) and decrease Errors a Minute (EAM) at the same time (SAM and EAM are discussed in detail on page 14).

If you make too many errors on a drill, for the next drill concentrate on accuracy. If your speed is too slow, concentrate on increasing strokes a minute.

Ten-Key Numeric Drill #1

	(A)	(B)	(C)	(D)	(E)
	9,067	634,825	127,434	29,727	128,496
	512,508	6,412	89,451	6,758	34,725
	83,583	87,519	201,985	343,261	2,933
25 strokes →	371,906	195,184	5,762	470,197	886,741
	889,457	65,432	72,581	8,429	56,487
	653,642	879,515	4,098	51,948	82,546
	652	54,267	91,013	16,423	6,545
	82,934	3,974	674,523	757,827	712,478
50 strokes →	2,603,749	1,927,128	1,266,847	1,684,570	1,910,951

	(F)	(G)	(H)	(I)	(J)
	125,367	344,513	39,418	4,687	42,132
	518,738	86,374	157,651	962,485	831,228
	7,666	85,622	722,489	31,621	57,582
25 strokes →	15,716	56,712	4,601	357,428	61,846
	731,249	128,469	8,427	96,487	46,252
	189,862	7,854	146,248	15,425	492,873
	44,487	95,223	87,984	184,531	71,742
	625	37,242	22,735	6,452	2,877
50 strokes →	1,633,710	842,009	1,189,553	1,659,116	1,606,532

	(K)	(L)	(M)	(N)	(O)
	93,172	814,984	15,469	609,305	812,592
	124,609	2,937	269,819	2,275	67,183
	3,312	65,034	4,785	367,011	1,551
25 strokes →	348,705	411,487	794,321	84,496	206,058
	9,152	96,504	135,091	570,322	4,602
	64,088	307,941	2,685	16,682	712,588
	204,913	8,553	44,167	1,934	439,966
	72,506	68,144	80,235	46,099	7,559
50 strokes →	920,457	1,775,584	1,346,572	1,698,124	2,252,099

CALCULATING STROKES A MINUTE (SAM) AND ERRORS A MINUTE (EAM)

After you complete the drill, calculate and record your scores as follows:

1. Strokes a Minute (SAM)

a. Count the number of strokes (numeric digits and function keys) that you completed. For example, if you completed the drill through the addend *128,469* in Problem G, the stroke count would be as follows:

Strokes

300	Problems A–F (50 x 6 = 300)
25	Problem G to the 25-strokes marker
7	Problem G for the addend *128,469* and the Add Key
332	Total Strokes

b. Divide your total number of strokes by 3 minutes to obtain your Strokes a Minute (SAM).

332	Total Strokes
÷ 3	3 minutes
111	Strokes a Minute (SAM)

2. Errors a Minute (EAM)

a. Compare your answer on the tape with the answer below each problem.

b. If your answer is different from the answer below the problem, compare each addend and circle each error on the tape.

c. Add the total number of errors in all problems. For example, if there were three errors in Problem C and one error in Problem E, there would be four total errors.

d. Divide your total number of errors by 3 minutes to obtain your Errors a Minute (EAM).

3. Go to the TKNDrill Record on page 118 and record your Total Strokes, Total Errors, SAM, and EAM. Follow the sample line and the instructions on page 118 to complete recording your scores.

➤ TEN-KEY NUMERIC DRILL #1, ATTEMPT #2

Complete the drill again following the procedure on page 13. Record your scores on page 118 for Attempt #2.

➤ TEN-KEY NUMERIC DRILL #1, ATTEMPT #3

Complete the drill again following the same procedure. Record your scores on page 118 for Attempt #3. Also, record your best score of the three attempts.

APPLICATION FOR YOUR LIFE
Touch Method

Learning the ten-key touch method will be a valuable asset for you. It is a skill that is transferable to other office equipment such as the ten-key numeric keypad on computer keyboards.

Job 4
Subtraction

LEARNING OBJECTIVES

1. Use the touch method to solve subtraction problems.
2. Increase Strokes a Minute (SAM) or decrease Errors a Minute (EAM) on the Ten-Key Numeric Drill (TKNDrill).

► WARM-UP DRILL: 7, 8, AND 9 KEYS

1. Review your ratings from Job 3 on the Technique Checklist, page 116.
2. Strive to improve techniques marked with a zero.
3. Work each problem until each answer matches the book's answer.

► SKILL BUILDER

How you strike the keys will determine your speed and accuracy. The Technique, Speed, and Accuracy Drills in the Appendix have been carefully designed so you will continuously improve your technique, which will improve your speed and accuracy. Work the following drills:

1. Technique Drills A–F, page 115.
2. Speed Drills A–E, page 114. Record your scores on the Speed Drill Record.
3. Accuracy Drills A–E, page 112.

SUBTRACTION

Locate the Subtract Key 27 . Strike the Subtract Key with the index finger if you use your left hand or with the little finger if you use your right hand. Keeping your other fingers on the home row, practice reaching to the Subtract Key three times *without* actually striking the key.

Warm-Up Drill: 7, 8, and 9 Keys
Keep your fingers curved over the keypad.

987	738	889	957	786
778	892	799	819	269
898	801	878	477	881
879	950	997	838	409
799	875	898	976	582
978	709	787	782	789
5,319	4,965	5,248	4,849	3,716

Subtraction

Strike the Subtract Key with your index finger.

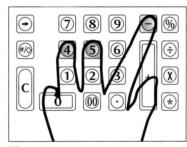

Illus. 4-A
Left-Hand Operation.

Strike the Subtract Key with your little finger.

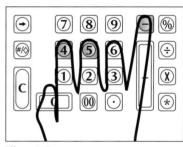

Illus. 4-B
Right-Hand Operation.

Subtraction is taking one number away from another number.

In subtraction, the number to be subtracted *from* is called the **minuend** and the number *to be subtracted* is called the **subtrahend**.

The answer is called the **remainder** or the **difference**.

85	**Minuend**
−23	**Subtrahend**
62	**Remainder** or **Difference**

Subtraction (continued)

Steps for Subtracting

Operation	Tape*	Display*
1. Clear the calculator.	0.CA	0
2. Enter the minuend (85).		85
3. Strike the Add Key.	85.+	85
4. Enter the subtrahend (23).		23
5. Strike the Subtract Key.	23.–	62
6. Strike the Total Key.	62.*	62

*Symbols may differ on your calculator.

1.	2.	3.	4.	5.
85	639	643	4,350	1,694
–23	–40	–471	–411	–1,052
62				

6.	7.	8.	9.	10.
639	2,461	5,391	10,397	37,540
–157	–932	–1,027	–650	–8,510
4,665	87	322	812	934
–910	–603	–489	–4,056	759
–1,159	71	2,265	877	–1,265
37	426	–77	–4,453	180
654	–130	104	892	–2,002

Credit Balances

11.	12.	13.	14.	15.
245	630	259	8,210	1,282
–487	–965	–753	–8,600	–3,977
–242				

Answers

1. 62
2.
3.
4.
5.
6.
7.
8.
9.
10.
11. –242
12.
13.
14.
15.

➤ **SUBTRACTION (continued)**
Work Problems 1–10 by following the **Steps for Subtracting** on the left.

➤ **CREDIT BALANCES**
When a larger number is subtracted from a smaller number, the answer will be a **credit balance**. Credit balances are usually preceded by or followed by a –, or printed in red ink.

Follow the **Steps for Subtracting** to work Problems 11–15. The answer (–242) will appear in the display window and print on the tape with a minus (–), or in red ink. Record your answers with a minus (–) sign.

➤ **TEN-KEY NUMERIC DRILL**
1. *Setting Your Goal.* Go to the TKNDrill Record, page 118, and set your TKNDrill goal for Job 4 following the instructions next to the TKNDrill Record, Item (4).
2. *Meeting Your Goal.* As you complete the drill, think about your goal on the TKNDrill Record. Strive only for speed or only for accuracy. Now, complete TKNDrill #1 on page 13.
3. *Recording Your Scores.* Go to the TKNDrill Record, page 118, and record your scores as you did in Job 3. If you reached your goal, circle it on the TKNDrill Record.

TECHNIQUE CHECKLIST
Complete the Technique Checklist on page 116. Compare your technique ratings for Job 3 with those for this job. Pay special attention to those items marked with a zero in the previous job. Did you improve?

Job 5
Review; Analyzing Progress; Setting Goals

LEARNING OBJECTIVES

1. Review addition and subtraction problems using the touch method.
2. Increase SAM or decrease EAM to prepare for the Ten-Key Numeric Test (TKNTest).

➤ WARM-UP DRILL: 1, 2, AND 3 KEYS

1. Review your ratings from Job 4 on the Technique Checklist, page 116.
2. Strive to improve techniques marked with a zero.
3. Work these drill problems in the usual manner.

➤ SKILL BUILDER

To improve your technique, speed, and accuracy, complete the following drills as you did in Job 4.

1. Technique Drills A–F, page 115.
2. Speed Drills A–E, page 114. Record your scores on the Speed Drill Record.
3. Accuracy Drills A–E, page 112.

➤ REVIEW OF JOBS 1–4

Complete Problems 1–15, which review Jobs 1–4.

NAME_____ DATE_____ PERIOD_____ GRADE_____

Warm-Up Drill: 1, 2, and 3 Keys

Do not pause between strokes.

231	321	136	193	263
131	213	925	524	932
321	131	871	207	541
213	212	401	316	710
112	323	502	182	258
323	112	603	423	123
1,331	1,312	3,438	1,845	2,827

Review of Jobs 1–4

Addition

1.	2.	3.	4.	5.
6,796	72,270	416	48	599
43,880	26,100	61,580	7,794	913
16	812,433	6,088	5,601	6,782
727	708	38,066	253	25,344
604,935	21,883	169	48,418	262
8,162	660	7,963	59	12,510

Subtraction

6.	7.	8.	9.	10.
5,039	6,001	4,098	2,353	5,460
−2,811	−5,328	−1,553	−647	−6,211

Addition and Subtraction

11.	12.	13.	14.	15.
2,938	8,725	792	9,405	870
−349	−6,145	−128	566	8,019
1,551	−854	1,436	−7,095	−2,412
−936	1,035	79	1,708	−3,648
7,232	534	−2,145	−5,115	86

Answers

1. _____
2. _____
3. _____
4. _____
5. _____
6. _____
7. _____
8. _____
9. _____
10. _____
11. _____
12. _____
13. _____
14. _____
15. _____

➤ **TEN-KEY NUMERIC DRILL**

Complete TKNDrill #1 on page 13.

If you completed Jobs 1–5 in less than five hours, repeat them until you complete five hours of practice. Do this before you take the TKNTest so that your scores can be compared with others who have completed five hours of practice.

Your teacher will administer the TKNTest.

TECHNIQUE CHECKLIST

Complete the Technique Checklist on page 116.

Compare your technique ratings for Job 4 with those for this job. Pay special attention to those items marked with a zero in the previous job. Did you improve?

ANALYZING PROGRESS AND SETTING GOALS

1. Answer Questions 1 and 2 on this page after analyzing your SAM pattern on the TKNDrill Graph—SAM, page 119.
2. Set SAM goals for Jobs 6–10 by answering Questions 3 and 4.
3. Answer Questions 5 and 6 after analyzing your EAM pattern on the TKNDrill Graph—EAM, page 119.
4. Set EAM goals for Jobs 6–10 by answering Questions 7 and 8.

STROKES A MINUTE (SAM)

1. Was there a steady increase in SAM on every drill from Jobs 3–5?

    Yes_____ No_____

    If No, list some reasons why.

    _____

    _____

    _____

2. How many SAM did you increase when comparing the TKNDrill in Job 3 with the TKNDrill in Job 5?

    SAM INCREASE_____

3. How many SAM do you believe you can get by Job 10?

    SAM_____

4. On the TKNTest after Job 10, how many SAM do you believe you can get?

    SAM_____

ERRORS A MINUTE (EAM)

5. Was your EAM .33 or less in:

    Job 3   Yes_____ No_____
    Job 4   Yes_____ No_____
    Job 5   Yes_____ No_____

6. In Jobs 3–5, if your EAM was not .33 or less, list some reasons why.

    _____

    _____

    _____

7. Do you believe you can keep EAM at .33 or less in Jobs 6–10?

    Yes_____ No_____

8. On the TKNTest after Job 10, do you believe you can get .33 EAM or less?

    Yes_____ No_____

TECHNIQUE, SPEED, AND ACCURACY

In business, your numerical work must be 100% accurate. You must strive to eliminate errors. Work problems a second time to verify your answers. The only time you are not striving for 100% accuracy is when you temporarily abandon accuracy with the intent of developing speed.

After the desired speed level is attained, practice again for accuracy and attempt to maintain the desired speed level. If accuracy is not good (more than .33 EAM), slow down to regain accuracy.

The Ten-Key Numeric Drill Record on page 118 will help measure your improvement as you progress through the jobs.

Good technique will improve both speed and accuracy. Whenever you have time, practice the Technique Drills on page 115.

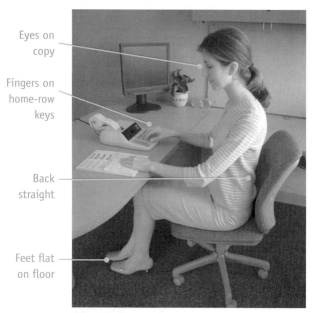

Eyes on copy

Fingers on home-row keys

Back straight

Feet flat on floor

Illus. 5-A
Practice correct posture.

Job 6

Non-Add Key; Decimal Point Key; Add Mode; Alignment of Decimals; Subtotal Key

LEARNING OBJECTIVES

1. Use the Non-Add Key to print problem numbers on the tape.
2. Use the Decimal Point Key and Subtotal Key by touch.
3. Use the Add Mode and Decimal Alignment features.

➤ **WARM-UP DRILL: 7, 8, AND 9 KEYS**

Complete the Warm-Up Drill following the usual procedure.

➤ **SKILL BUILDER**

To improve your technique, speed, and accuracy, complete the following drills:

1. Technique Drills A–F, page 115.
2. Speed Drills A–E, page 114. Record your scores on the Speed Drill Record.
3. Accuracy Drills A–E, page 112.

➤ **NON-ADD KEY**

Striking the Non-Add Key [21] will print a number on the tape but will not add the number into the total. The Non-Add Key can identify an employee number, problem number, or date. To work Problems 1–6:

1. Clear the calculator.
2. Print the problem number on the tape as you work each problem. For example, strike the 1 Key and the Non-Add Key to print "#1".
3. Prove your answers (as explained on page 111) and record them in the Answers column.
4. Number all future problems, except the TKN-Drills and TKNTests, unless instructed otherwise.

NAME_____ DATE_____ PERIOD_____ GRADE_____

Warm-Up Drill: 7, 8, and 9 Keys

Keep your eyes on the problem in the book.

997	827	879	759	678
788	981	788	284	159
797	703	979	903	772
899	590	798	177	109
989	784	897	838	483
787	609	978	497	789
5,257	4,494	5,319	3,458	2,990

Non-Add Key

1.

| 59 |
| 35 |
| 14 |
| 93 |
| 28 |
| 40 |
| 56 |
| 87 |
| 412 |

```
#1        0.  CA
        59.  +
        35.  +
        14.  +
        93.  +
        28.  +
        40.  +
        56.  +
        87.  +
       412.  *
```

Illus. 6-A
Sample Tape for Problem 1.

Answers

1. _____412_____
2. _____
3. _____
4. _____
5. _____
6. _____

2.	**3.**	**4.**	**5.**	**6.**
34	275	203	157	584
47	30	64	743	331
76	447	489	36	233
69	532	95	698	227
91	83	503	84	164
18	189	314	407	910
83	64	47	72	413
35	16	756	201	796

Decimal Point Key

#7	0. CA
23.50	+
6.07	+
4.19	+
2.39	+
51.74	+
0.81	+
0.22	+
69.75	+
42.04	+
7.31	+
208.02	*

Illus. 6-B
Sample Tape for Problem 7.

7.	8.	9.
23.50	2.417	36.100
6.07	51.788	19.747
4.19	3.052	3.256
2.39	.189	.160
51.74	.600	.245
.81	.657	4.691
.22	5.129	2.113
69.75	9.101	.512
42.04	3.288	5.889
7.31	.497	2.635
208.02		

Answers

7.	208.02
8.	
9.	
10.	689.11
11.	
12.	
13.	
14.	

Add Mode

10.	11.	12.	13.	14.
108.45	88.45	2,017.65	542.64	53.00
28.79	126.06	285.49	31.89	283.45
66.12	3,072.31	3.00	685.50	2,091.16
7.13	92.24	.14	1,293.77	.37
4.00	5.87	379.88	.92	409.52
9.56	63.90	46.97	48.01	7.70
407.21	.72	22.00	205.35	7.19
18.67	40.18	362.47	8.67	63.28
33.41	5,912.23	1.99	.29	.05
5.77	8.59	3.86	3,007.41	146.22
689.11				

➤ DECIMAL POINT KEY

Strike the Decimal Point Key [8] with the index finger if you use your left hand or with the ring finger if you use your right hand. To work Problems 7–9:

1. Clear the calculator.
2. Set the Decimal Place Selector [7] according to the number of decimal places required in each problem. For example, all the addends in Problem 7 have two decimal places, so the Decimal Place Selector should be set at *2*.
3. Enter the addends, striking the Decimal Point Key as the decimal occurs in each number.
   a. If the last digit (or digits) after the decimal point is zero (23.50), it is not necessary to enter a zero.
   b. If a zero after the decimal point is followed by a number (6.07), enter the zero.
4. Prove and record your answers as explained on page 111.

➤ ADD MODE

The Add Mode [2] is a decimal setting which eliminates the need to strike the Decimal Point Key. When in the Add Mode, the calculator automatically places the decimal point at two places in addition or subtraction problems.

The Add Mode is usually on the Decimal Place Selector and labeled "+" or "ADD (2)." (For calculators that have an Add Mode separate from the Decimal Place Selector, refer to the operating manual.)

When in the Add Mode, all numbers in the addend must be entered. For example, in Problem 7, the zero in *23.50 must* be entered. If the zero is not entered, the number will be incorrectly printed as *2.35.* To work Problems 10–14:

1. Engage the Add Mode. Enter the numbers, remembering it is not necessary to strike the Decimal Point Key.
2. Prove and record your answers.

NAME_____ DATE_____ PERIOD_____ GRADE_____

ALIGNMENT OF DECIMALS

You can get the correct answer to a problem without aligning the decimals on the tape, or you can set the function keys of your calculator so that decimals will be aligned on the tape. Work the Sample Problem using the procedure for Unaligned Decimals below. Work the Sample Problem again using the procedure for Aligned Decimals.

➤ UNALIGNED DECIMALS

Work the Sample Problem:

1. Set the Decimal Rounding Selector ⑨ at *Float* (usually an "F" on the Decimal Place Selector).
2. a. If the last digit after the decimal point is zero (15.20), do not enter the zero.
   b. If a zero after the decimal point is followed by a number (1.02), enter the zero.
3. Enter the addends, striking the Decimal Point Key as the decimal occurs in each number.

➤ ALIGNED DECIMALS

Work the Sample Problem to align decimals at 3 places:

1. Set the Decimal Rounding Selector at *5/4*.
2. Set the Decimal Place Selector to accommodate the addend in the problem with the most number of decimal places (three decimal places for the addend *6.239*).
3. Follow Steps 2 and 3 above for Unaligned Decimals.

To work Problems 15–20:

1. Work the problems using the procedure for Unaligned Decimals.
2. Work the problems again using the procedure for Aligned Decimals.
3. Prove and record your answers.

Alignment of Decimals

6.239 Sample
15.20 Problem
1.02

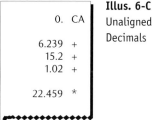

Illus. 6-C
Unaligned
Decimals

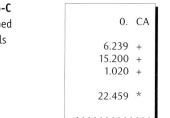

Illus. 6-D
Aligned
Decimals

15.	16.	17.
6,948	143.63	2,115.74
32.974	40.1	126.099
5.26	63.785	643.58
890.5	38.08	17.41
2.18	21.45	808.332
100.663	447.12	900.21
8.4	316.205	6.5
627.01	948.77	954.203
77.5	0.9	989.3
0.49	5.13	0.07
8,692.977		

Answers

15. 8,692.977

16. _____

17. _____

18. _____

19. _____

20. _____

18. 614.12 + 787.356 + 7.5 + 76.09 + 341.5 +   = _____
89.67 + 6,088.549 + 91.445 + 321.07 + .8

19. 968.72 + 0.35 + 71.99 + 2.06 + .3 +   = _____
45.51 + 800.27 + 6.83 + .49 + 75.0

20. 18.22 + 908.55 + 32.07 + 6.1 + 7.809 +   = _____
665.143 + 77.28 + .7 + 43.65 + 706.52

Subtotal Key

```
#21        0. CA

     452.09 +
       3.76 +
     180.22 +
      94.35 +
      71.61 +
     802.03 ◊

     632.92 +
      58.74 +
      20.13 +

   1,513.82 *
```

Illus. 6-E
Sample Tape for
Problem 21.

21.	**22.**
452.09	255.88
3.76	737.99
180.22	2.90
94.35	86.77
71.61	381.51
802.03 S	794.12
632.92	S
58.74	675.91
20.13	532.91
1,513.82 T	T

Answers

21.	S	802.03
	T	1,513.82
22.	S	
	T	
23.	S	
	T	
24.	S	
	T	
25.	S	
	T	
26.	S	
	T	
27.	S	
	T	
28.	S	
	T	
29.	S	
	T	
30.	S	
	T	

23.	**24.**	**25.**	**26.**
26.41	244.67	73.24	44.82
721.89	3.12	189.85	649.31
10.63	89.19	6.10	.65
41.26	5.26	47.39	70.20
S	S	.02	S
818.72	76.67	S	4.89
455.43	1.92	9.71	5.83
61.76	503.83	240.06	461.78
23.89	.24	35.28	107.36
T	T	T	T

27.	**28.**	**29.**	**30.**
8.60	46.63	27.93	328.22
44.86	7.16	83.56	3.30
588.40	863.97	3.17	50.24
11.43	S	S	41.00
S	33.97	49.93	1.67
364.47	171.20	56.20	S
7.84	80.99	574.09	813.50
95.75	27.93	364.08	0.10
0.05	63.00	7.21	93.53
T	T	T	T

➤ SUBTOTAL KEY

A **subtotal** is a total of *part* of a group of numbers. Strike the Subtotal Key [26] with the index finger if you use your left hand or with the little finger if you use your right hand. To work Problems 21–30:

1. Clear the calculator.
2. Set the Decimal Place Selector at *2*, or use the Add Mode.
3. Add the numbers until there is a space for a subtotal, indicated by the S.
4. Locate the Subtotal Key on your calculator. (The Subtotal Key may be marked with an S or ◊.)
5. Strike the Subtotal Key and record the subtotal in the space provided (802.03).
6. Continue to add numbers until there is a space in the problem for the Total, indicated by T, and strike the Total Key (1,513.82).
7. Prove and record your answers.

➤ TEN-KEY NUMERIC DRILL

Complete TKNDrill #2 on page 117 as you have done for TKNDrill #1.

TECHNIQUE CHECKLIST

Complete the Technique Checklist on page 116 in the usual manner.

PROCEDURE FOR FUTURE JOBS

In future calculating jobs, you will not always be reminded to clear the calculator, set the operational keys, prove and verify answers, or record answers in the Answers column.

Job 7
Multiplication

LEARNING OBJECTIVES
1. Use the touch method to solve multiplication problems.
2. Estimate answers for multiplication problems.
3. Use the Constant feature to solve multiplication problems.

➤ WARM-UP DRILL: 0, 00, AND DECIMAL POINT KEYS
Work the Warm-up Drill problems in the usual manner.

➤ SKILL BUILDER
To improve your technique, speed, and accuracy, complete the following drills:
1. Technique Drills A–F, page 115.
2. Speed Drills A–E, page 114. Record your scores on the Speed Drill Record.
3. Accuracy Drills A–E, page 112.

➤ MULTIPLICATION
The **multiplicand** (the number to be multiplied) and the **multiplier** (the number of times to multiply) are **factors** of a multiplication problem. The answer to a multiplication problem is called the **product**. Whether the factors are whole numbers, decimals, or fractions, follow the same procedure for multiplying.

Set the Print Selector at *Off*. It is not necessary to use the print feature to work short problems involving few calculations.

Work Problems 1–8 by following the **Steps for Multiplying**.

NAME_____ DATE_____ PERIOD_____ GRADE_____

Warm-Up Drill: 0, 00, and Decimal Point Keys
Set the Decimal Place Selector correctly.

8.762	2.090	8.900	3.609	4.902
4.003	7.060	6.704	2.405	2.007
5.010	1.080	8.030	7.009	6.000
2.068	3.005	2.019	8.052	1.400
3.007	4.018	4.500	1.000	8.000
1.405	1.810	3.014	3.600	2.043
24.255	19.063	33.167	25.675	24.352

Multiplication

$$
\begin{array}{rl}
8 & \text{Multiplicand} \\
\times\ 5 & \text{Multiplier} \\
\hline
40 & \text{Product}
\end{array} \Big\} \text{Factors}
$$

Steps for Multiplying

Operation	Tape	Display
1. Enter the multiplicand (8).		8
2. Strike the Multiply Key [20].	8. ×	8
3. Enter the multiplier (5).		5
4. Strike the Equals Key [11].	5. = 40. *	40

Answers

1. _____ 40
2. _____
3. _____
4. _____
5. _____
6. _____
7. _____
8. _____

1. 8 × 5 = _____ 40
2. 8,970 × 42 = _____
3. 3,167 × 68 = _____
4. 409 × 26 = _____
5. 5,788 × 640 = _____
6. 43,102 × 203 = _____
7. 6,429 × 81 = _____
8. 7,785 × 136 = _____

Estimating Answers

		Rounded Factors	Estimated Product	Calculator Product
9.	42 x 11 =	40 x 10	400	462
10.	40 x 28 =			
11.	2,532 x 37 =			
12.	7,542 x 234 =			
13.	981 x 770 =			

Decimals in Multiplication: Unrounded Products

> **424.13 x 5.7 = 2,417.541**
> 2 decimal places in   +   1 decimal place in
> multiplicand (.13)   multiplier (.7)
>   = 3 total decimal places in product (.541)

14.	424.13 x 5.7 =	2,417.541
15.	285.56 x 43.8 =	
16.	30.893 x 6.4 =	
17.	542.31 x 347.9 =	
18.	84.10 x 87.9 =	
19.	68.12 x 53.4 =	
20.	152.326 x 9.9 =	
21.	5,468.11 x .53 =	
22.	57.4 x 27.3 =	
23.	629.58 x 95.20 =	

Answers

9.	462
10.	
11.	
12.	
13.	
14.	2,417.541
15.	
16.	
17.	
18.	
19.	
20.	
21.	
22.	
23.	

➤ **ESTIMATING ANSWERS**

Estimating your answers can help you find errors. To work Problems 9–13:

1. *Mentally* round the factors to the closest numbers that are easy to multiply mentally (multiples of ten). Record them in the Rounded Factors column (42 = 40 and 11 = 10).

2. *Mentally* multiply the rounded factors and record the product in the Estimated Product column (40 x 10 = 400).

3. Multiply the unrounded factors on your calculator and record the product in the Calculator Product column (42 x 11 = 462).

4. If your estimated product (400) and calculator product (462) are not close to each other, estimate and calculate the answer again. Record the correct calculator product in the Answers column.

➤ **DECIMALS IN MULTIPLICATION: UNROUNDED PRODUCTS**

Products can be **unrounded**. This means the answer will be carried out to the total number of decimal places in the multiplicand and the multiplier. The Float Setting (usually an "F") on the Decimal Place Selector 7 will automatically cause the decimal point to "float" in the product for the total number of places in the multiplicand and multiplier.

To work Problems 14–23:

1. Set the Decimal Place Selector to *F* (Float Setting).

2. Work the problems, entering the decimal points in their proper places in the multiplicand and the multiplier.

NAME_____ DATE_____ PERIOD_____ GRADE_____

➤ DECIMALS IN MULTIPLICATION: ROUNDED PRODUCTS

In most business calculations, a two-place decimal in the answer is sufficient. Unless otherwise instructed, round the answers to two decimal places for all problems in this book.

To round a product to two decimal places, at least three decimal places are needed in the answer. If the third decimal is 5 or more, the second decimal is increased by one. If the third decimal is 4 or less, the second decimal does not change. The *5/4* position on the Decimal Rounding Selector 9 automatically rounds answers to the decimal place specified by the Decimal Place Selector setting.

To work Problems 24–33:
1. Set the Decimal Rounding Selector at *5/4* and the Decimal Place Selector at *2*.
2. Multiply the factors in each problem (.81 x .4 = .32) and record your answers in the Answers column.

➤ ESTIMATING ANSWERS WITH DECIMALS

Since many business calculations involve decimals, it is important that you know how to estimate answers with decimals.

To work Problems 34–40:
1. Round the factors to whole numbers (7 x 5) and record them in the Rounded Factors column. *Mentally* multiply the rounded factors and record the product (35) in the Estimated Product column.
2. Multiply the unrounded factors on your calculator. Round the product to two decimal places and record the product in the Calculator Product column and in the Answers column (31.49).
3. Repeat the problem if the calculator product is not near your estimated product.

Decimals in Multiplication: Rounded Products

$$\begin{array}{r} 6.53 \\ \times\ .2 \\ \hline 1.306 \end{array} = 1.31$$

The second decimal increases if the third decimal is 5 or greater.

$$\begin{array}{r} 4.17 \\ \times\ .9 \\ \hline 3.753 \end{array} = 3.75$$

The second decimal does not change if the third decimal is 4 or less.

24. .81 x .4 = _____ .32

25. 47.1 x 9.33 = _____

26. 63.552 x 4.25 = _____

27. 714.3 x 821.56 = _____

28. 218.47 x 10.3 = _____

29. 465.78 x 299.23 = _____

30. 5.2 x 348.611 = _____

31. 891.8 x .351 = _____

32. 637.51 x 29.4 = _____

33. 37.43 x 61.08 = _____

Estimating Answers with Decimals

		Rounded Factors	Estimated Product	Calculator Product
34.	6.70 x 4.7 =	7 x 5	35	31.49
35.	24.8 x 5.13 =			
36.	21.35 x 3.84 =			
37.	5.571 x 39.7 =			
38.	3.82 x 6.771 =			
39.	81.38 x 1.09 =			
40.	4.92 x 9.225 =			

APPLICATION FOR YOUR LIFE | Estimating

You have $10 to spend for groceries. Bread costs $2.55; butter, $1.90; milk, $3.41; and eggs, $2.03. Estimate the total to find out if you have enough money to purchase all of these items.

Answers

24.	.32
25.	
26.	
27.	
28.	
29.	
30.	
31.	
32.	
33.	
34.	31.49
35.	
36.	
37.	
38.	
39.	
40.	

Constant Multiplication

Steps for Constant Multiplication

Operation	Tape	Display
1. Engage the Constant Key 6 .*		K
2. Enter the constant factor (20).		20
3. Strike the Multiply Key.**	20. x	20
4. Enter the nonconstant factor (14).		14
5. Strike the Equals Key to obtain the product.	14. = 280. *	280
6. Enter the next nonconstant factor (7).		7
7. Strike the Equals Key to obtain the next product.	7. = 140. *	140
8. Repeat Steps 6 and 7 for the remaining nonconstant factors.		

* Omit this step if your machine does not have a Constant Key. On some calculators, Step 2 must be completed before Step 1.

** Strike the Multiply Key twice if your calculator does not automatically retain a constant.

Overflow

Steps for Overflow

Operation	Tape	Display
1. Enter the multiplicand (132,354,761).		132,354,761
2. Strike the Multiply Key.	132,354,761. x	132,354,761
3. Enter the multiplier (289,036).		289,036
4. Strike the Equals Key.*	E 3,825.529070*	E 3,825.529070
5. Clear the calculator.	0. CA	0.

* Your answer may differ depending on how your machine calculates overflows.

50. 132,354,761 x 289,036 =   E 3,825.529070

51. 483,951,322 x 249,322 = _____

Group A
41. 14 x 20 = _____280_____
42. 7 x 20 = _____140_____
43. 9 x 20 = _____

Group B
44. 11 x 52 = _____
45. 11 x 68 = _____
46. 11 x 39 = _____

Group C
47. 77 x 48 = _____
48. 251 x 48 = _____
49. 89 x 48 = _____

Answers

41. _____280
42. _____140
43. _____
44. _____
45. _____
46. _____
47. _____
48. _____
49. _____
50. E 3,825.529070
51. _____

➤ CONSTANT MULTIPLICATION

A **constant** is a number that appears more than once in a series of multiplication problems. A constant can be the multiplier or the multiplicand. However, in either case, the constant must be the first number entered when working constant multiplication problems.

Work Problems 41–49 using the **Steps for Constant Multiplication**. When a new constant is entered, the previous constant is automatically erased.

➤ OVERFLOW

An **overflow** occurs when you attempt an entry or get an answer exceeding the capacity of the operating register, such as 12 digits. Some calculators will display or print as many digits as its capacity will allow. Others will indicate the overflow as an E, a series of red dots, or some other error symbol.

Work Problems 50 and 51 by following the **Steps for Overflow**.

➤ TEN-KEY NUMERIC DRILL

Complete TKNDrill #2 on page 117 in the usual manner.

TECHNIQUE CHECKLIST

Complete the Technique Checklist on page 116 in the usual manner.

Job 8
Division

NAME_____ DATE_____ PERIOD_____ GRADE_____

LEARNING OBJECTIVES
1. Use the touch method to solve division problems.
2. Estimate answers for division problems.
3. Determine averages.
4. Use the Constant feature to solve division problems.
5. Solve chain division problems.

➤ WARM-UP DRILL: 1, 4, AND 7 KEYS
Work the Warm-Up Drill problems in the usual manner.

➤ SKILL BUILDER
To improve your technique, speed, and accuracy, complete the following drills:
1. Technique Drills A–F, page 115.
2. Speed Drills A–E, page 114. Record your scores on the Speed Drill Record.
3. Accuracy Drills A–E, page 112.

➤ DIVISION
The **dividend** (the number to be divided) and the **divisor** (the number that the dividend is to be divided by) are the parts of a division problem. The answer to a division problem is called the **quotient**. (See the chart showing **Three Ways of Writing Division Problems**.)

Set the Print Selector at *Off*. It is not necessary to use the print feature to work short problems involving few calculations.

Work Problems 1–10 by following the **Steps for Dividing**.

Warm-Up Drill: 1, 4, and 7 Keys
Strike each key firmly and quickly.

717	471	497	451	174
477	141	784	134	451
147	741	240	414	761
714	717	417	477	137
441	147	497	746	781
174	447	164	431	491
2,670	2,664	2,599	2,653	2,795

Division
Three Ways of Writing Division Problems

$\dfrac{\text{Quotient}}{\text{Divisor})\overline{\text{Dividend}}}$	Dividend ÷ Divisor = Quotient	$\dfrac{\text{Dividend}}{\text{Divisor}}$ = Quotient
$22\overline{)307}$ with 13.95 above	307 ÷ 22 = 13.95	$\dfrac{307}{22} = 13.95$

Steps for Dividing

Operation	Tape	Display
1. Enter the dividend (307).		307
2. Strike the Divide Key [÷].	307. ÷	307
3. Enter the divisor (22).		22
4. Strike the Equals Key.	22. = 13.95 *	13.95

1. $22\overline{)307}$ (13.95 above)

2. $40\overline{)428}$

3. $3,258 \div 417 =$ _____

4. $7,925 \div 104 =$ _____

5. $1,947 \div 36 =$ _____

6. $\dfrac{2,461}{44} =$ _____

7. $\dfrac{837}{42} =$ _____

8. $\dfrac{5,224}{49} =$ _____

9. $\dfrac{24,000}{2,400} =$ _____

10. $\dfrac{20,341}{480} =$ _____

Answers
1. ___13.95___
2. _____
3. _____
4. _____
5. _____
6. _____
7. _____
8. _____
9. _____
10. _____

Decimals in Division: Unrounded Quotients

```
   44. 44444444
9 )400
```

11. 400 ÷ 9 = __44.44444444__

12. 438 ÷ 71 = _____

13. 2,183 ÷ 54 = _____

14. 3,519 ÷ 284 = _____

15. 966 ÷ 839 = _____

16. 4,816 ÷ 639 = _____

17. 510 ÷ 9 = _____

18. 3,996 ÷ 201 = _____

19. 1,995 ÷ 17 = _____

Decimals in Division: Rounded Quotients

```
   44. 44
9 )400
```

20. 400 ÷ 9 = __44.44__

21. 5,721 ÷ 45 = _____

22. 1,732 ÷ 538 = _____

23. 5,173 ÷ 3,264 = _____

24. 2,018 ÷ 45 = _____

25. 16,341 ÷ 485 = _____

26. 934 ÷ 32 = _____

27. 4,730 ÷ 862 = _____

28. 8,007 ÷ 96 = _____

Answers

11. __44.44444444__

12. _____

13. _____

14. _____

15. _____

16. _____

17. _____

18. _____

19. _____

20. __44.44__

21. _____

22. _____

23. _____

24. _____

25. _____

26. _____

27. _____

28. _____

➤ DECIMALS IN DIVISION: UNROUNDED QUOTIENTS

Just as products can be unrounded in multiplication problems, quotients can be unrounded in division problems. The Float Setting will automatically cause the decimal point to "float" in the quotient to the total number of places in your calculator's register.

To work Problems 11–19:

1. Set the Print Selector at *Off*.
2. Set the Decimal Place Selector at *Float*.
3. Enter the dividend (400) and strike the Divide Key.
4. Enter the divisor (9) and strike the Equals Key to get the quotient (44.44444444). The number of decimal places in the quotient will vary according to the capacity of your calculator's register.

➤ DECIMALS IN DIVISION: ROUNDED QUOTIENTS

As in multiplication, your calculator can automatically round the quotient to any of several different decimal places. Unless otherwise instructed, when working division problems, record your answers rounded to two decimal places as explained in **Rounded Products** on page 25.

To work Problems 20–28:

1. Set the Print Selector at *Off*.
2. Set the Decimal Rounding Selector at *5/4*.
3. Set the Decimal Place Selector at *2*.
4. Divide the dividend by the divisor (400 ÷ 9). The quotient will be rounded to two decimal places (44.44).

DECIMALS IN DIVIDENDS AND DIVISORS

Enter decimals in the proper positions in dividends and divisors. Your calculator will automatically place the decimal in the proper place in the quotient.

NAME_____ DATE_____ PERIOD_____ GRADE_____

► ESTIMATING ANSWERS IN DIVISION

Examine each quotient to be sure the answer seems reasonable.

To work Problems 29–36:

1. Set the Print Selector at *Off*.
2. *Mentally* round the dividend and the divisor to whole numbers so that you can easily divide them mentally (31.845 to 32 and 4.2 to 4).
3. *Mentally* divide the rounded dividend by the rounded divisor (32 ÷ 4 = 8).
4. Work the original problem with your calculator, and round the answer to three decimal places (7.582).
5. Compare your estimated answer (8) with the calculator answer (7.582). If your calculator answer is not reasonable in comparison with the estimated answer, work the problem again and check the decimal point placement.

► AVERAGES AND ITEM COUNT SELECTOR

To find the average of a problem, calculate the total; then divide by the number of addends in the problem.

The Item Count Selector 14 is used to count and print the number of addends and/or subtrahends in a problem.

To work Problems 37–39:

1. Set the Print Selector at *On*.
2. Engage the Item Count Selector.
3. Set the Decimal Place Selector at *2*, or use the Add Mode.
4. Enter the addends and strike the Total Key. The number of addends will be recorded to the left of the total. (See the sample tape for Problem 37.)
5. Strike the Divide Key.
6. Enter the number of addends in the problem.
7. Strike the Equals Key to get the average.

Estimating Answers in Division

29.	31.845	÷	4.2	=	7.582
30.	19.194	÷	8.5	=	
31.	209.183	÷	42.25	=	
32.	489.55	÷	61	=	
33.	374.85	÷	36.2	=	
34.	548.139	÷	264	=	
35.	736.14	÷	65.89	=	
36.	526.77	÷	237.55	=	

Averages and Item Count Selector

Illus. 8-A
Sample Tape for Problem 37.

```
#37         0. CA

   28.70 +
  691.09 +
  724.51 +
  890.03 +
  521.64 +
   42.67 +
  197.80 +
  204.48 +
  366.59 +
   78.31 +
   40.25 +
7,279.11 +
012
11,065.18 *

11,065.18 ÷
      12 =
  922.10
```

	37.	**38.**	**39.**
	28.70	15.36	120.86
	691.09	641.35	923.16
	724.51	254.19	89.40
	890.03	624.86	995.28
	521.64	106.41	243.68
	42.67	87.26	780.31
	197.80	822.30	528.24
	204.48	467.15	477.10
	366.59	274.23	93.45
	78.31	69.47	899.34
	40.25	246.19	446.50
	7,279.11	90.78	167.18
Total a.	11,065.18	a.	a.
Average b.	922.10	b.	b.

Answers

29.	7.582
30.	
31.	
32.	
33.	
34.	
35.	
36.	
37a.	11,065.18
b.	922.10
38a.	
b.	
39a.	
b.	

Constant Divisors

Steps for Constant Division

Operation	Tape	Display
1. Engage the Constant Key.*		K
2. Enter the constant factor (5).**		5
3. Strike the Divide Key.***	5. ÷	5
4. Enter the nonconstant factor (40).		40
5. Strike the Equals Key to obtain the quotient.	40. = 8. *	8
6. Enter the next nonconstant factor (120).		120
7. Strike the Equals Key to obtain the next quotient.	120 = 24. *	24
8. Repeat Steps 6 and 7 for the remaining nonconstant factors.		

  * Omit this step if your calculator does not have a Constant Key. On some calculators, Step 2 must be completed before Step 1.

 ** On some calculators, Steps 2 and 4 must be reversed.

*** Strike the Divide Key twice if your calculator does not automatically retain a constant.

40.	40	÷	5	=	8.00
41.	120	÷	5	=	24.00
42.	550	÷	5	=	
43.	695	÷	5	=	

44.	871	÷	26	=	
45.	2,445	÷	26	=	
46.	5,226	÷	26	=	
47.	5,284	÷	26	=	

Chain Division

48. 329 ÷ 17 ÷ 6 = 3.23

49. 5,505 ÷ 50 ÷ 5 =

50. 70,415 ÷ 43 ÷ 716 =

51. 348 ÷ 24 ÷ 8 =

52. 9,411 ÷ 428 ÷ 375 =

53. 789 ÷ 238 ÷ 2 =

54. 3,254 ÷ 391 ÷ 4 =

55. 6,540 ÷ 200 ÷ 4 =

Answers

40.	8.00
41.	24.00
42.	
43.	
44.	
45.	
46.	
47.	
48.	3.23
49.	
50.	
51.	
52.	
53.	
54.	
55.	

➤ CONSTANT DIVISORS

Your calculator solves **constant division** problems similar to the procedure for constant multiplication. However, in division, the constant must always be the divisor. The constant cannot be a dividend.

To work Problems 40–47:

1. Set the Print Selector at *On*.
2. Round answers to two decimal places.
3. Work Problems 40–47 following the **Steps for Constant Division**. When a new constant is entered, the previous constant is automatically erased.

➤ CHAIN DIVISION

When a division problem contains more than one divisor, the process is called **chain division**.

To work Problems 48–55:

1. Set the Print Selector at *Off*.
2. Round answers to two decimal places.
3. Enter the dividend (329) and strike the Divide Key.
4. Enter the first divisor (17) and strike the Divide Key. (On some calculators, you must strike the Equals Key before striking the Divide Key.)
5. Enter the second divisor (6) and strike the Equals Key (3.23).

If your calculator does not perform chain division as described in Steps 1–5, consult your operating manual or instructor.

➤ TEN-KEY NUMERIC DRILL

Complete TKNDrill #2 on page 117 in the usual manner.

TECHNIQUE CHECKLIST

Complete the Technique Checklist on page 116 in the usual manner.

NAME_____ DATE_____ PERIOD_____ GRADE_____

LEARNING OBJECTIVES

1. Use the memory register in solving business problems.
2. Use the Grand Total Key in addition problems.

➤ WARM-UP DRILL: 2, 5, AND 8 KEYS

Work these drill problems in the usual manner.

MEMORY REGISTER

Numbers can be entered into the **memory register** to be stored, added, or subtracted. Storing numbers in memory permits you to complete problems more efficiently. The total can be recalled repeatedly and placed in the **operating register** where it can be added, subtracted, multiplied, and divided. The total can also be recalled and cleared simultaneously from the memory register.

➤ MEMORY-PLUS KEY

The Memory-Plus Key 17 adds a number to the memory register.

Set the Print Selector at *On* and work the problem below by following the **Steps for Memory Plus**.

$$2 + 9 = 11$$
$$5 + 8 = \underline{13}$$
$$\underline{24} \text{ Memory Total}$$

To work Problems 1–4 on the next page:
1. Clear the operating register and memory register by striking the Clear-All Key.
2. Total the addends for Problem 1 and compare your sum with the sum below the problem.
3. Add the sum to the memory register by striking the Memory-Plus Key.

Warm-Up Drill: 2, 5, and 8 Keys

Keep your fingers curved over the keypad.

225	852	252	508	802
852	288	542	265	585
585	528	852	828	282
882	585	625	752	838
528	222	250	598	295
258	582	518	425	275
3,330	3,057	3,039	3,376	3,077

Memory-Plus Key

Steps for Memory Plus

Operation	Tape*	Display*
1. To clear the operating register and memory register, strike the Clear-All Key.**	0. CA	0
2. Enter the first addend (2) and strike the Add Key.	2. +	2
3. Enter the second addend (9) and strike the Add Key.	9. +	11
4. Strike the Total Key.	11. *	11
5. Strike the Memory-Plus Key 17.	11. M+	M 11
6. Enter the first addend (5) and strike the Add Key.	5. +	M 5
7. Enter the second addend (8) and strike the Add Key.	8. +	M 13
8. Strike the Total Key.	13. *	M 13
9. Strike the Memory-Plus Key.	13. M+	M 13
10. Strike the Memory-Recall (Total) Key 18.	24. M*	24

* On some calculators, the symbols may differ.

** On some calculators, it may be necessary to strike another key.

Memory-Plus Key (continued)

1.	2.	3.	4.
5,312	729	9,244	
1,564	6,858	572	Memory
6,521	432	381	Total
4,687	826	783	
18,084 +	+	=	

Memory-Minus Key

5.	6.	7.	8.
48,520	273	7,680	
3,459	7,400	1,465	Memory
1,576	6,448	4,837	Total
4,081	3,159	9,122	
–	–	=	

Grand Total Key

9.		10.		11.	
481.06		943.77		190.26	
224.53		569.47		42.31	
90.78		19.23			T
796.37	T	408.29		102.31	
726.13			T	225.49	
480.97		789.44		17.54	
55.32		123.89		9,257.37	
1,262.42	T		T		T
560.97		96.43		51.32	
62.41		323.61		852.36	
623.38	T		T		T
2,682.17	GT		GT		GT

Answers

1.		18,084
2.		
3.		
4.		
5.		
6.		
7.		
8.		
9.	T	796.37
	T	1,262.42
	T	623.38
	GT	2,682.17
10.	T	
	T	
	T	
	GT	
11.	T	
	T	
	T	
	GT	

➤ **MEMORY-PLUS KEY (continued)**

4. Clear the operating register before adding the next group of addends in Problem 2 by striking the Total Key. Do not clear the memory until you have calculated the Memory Total.

5. Repeat Steps 2–4 for each group of numbers and record your answers below the problems.

6. To obtain the Memory Total, strike the Memory-Recall (Total) Key 18.

➤ **MEMORY-MINUS KEY**

The Memory-Minus Key 16 subtracts a number from the memory register.

To work Problems 5–8, follow the instructions above, but subtract the sums of Problems 6 and 7 from the total in the memory register by striking the Memory-Minus Key.

➤ **GRAND TOTAL KEY**

A **grand total** is the sum of two or more totals. The grand total prints on the tape when you strike the Grand Total Key 13. If your calculator has a Grand Total Lever, set it at the Grand Total position. If your calculator does not calculate grand totals, go directly to Problem 12.

To work Problems 9–11:

1. Clear the calculator. Set the Decimal Place Selector at *2*, or use the Add Mode. Set the Decimal Rounding Selector at *5/4*.

2. Add the numbers until there is a space for a total, indicated by T. Strike the Total Key and record the answer in the space provided (796.37).

3. Continue to add numbers and get totals (1,262.42 and 623.38) until there is a space in the problem for the grand total, indicated by GT. Strike the Grand Total Key (2,682.17).

NAME_____DATE_____PERIOD_____GRADE_____

➤ MULTIPLICATION AND MEMORY

To work Problems 12–30:

1. Clear the operating register and the memory register.
2. Enter the multiplicand and strike the Multiply Key.
3. Enter the multiplier. Strike the Memory-Plus Key to enter the product into the memory.
4. Record the product.
5. Unlike addition and subtraction using memory, it is not necessary to clear the operating register before entering the next problem. When you strike the first key for the next multiplicand, the product automatically clears from the operating register.
6. Repeat Steps 2–4 for each set of factors.
7. Strike the Memory-Recall (Total) Key to obtain the Memory Total.

➤ DIVISION AND MEMORY

To work Problems 31–45:

1. Clear the operating register and the memory register.
2. Enter the dividend and strike the Divide Key.
3. Enter the divisor. Strike the Memory-Plus Key to enter the quotient into the memory.
4. Record the quotient.
5. It is not necessary to clear the operating register before entering the next problem.
6. Repeat Steps 2–4 for each set of factors.
7. Strike the Memory-Recall (Total) Key to obtain the Memory Total.

TWO MEMORY REGISTERS

Some calculators have two memory registers which allow accumulation of two different sets of numbers. Numbers can be entered into the second memory register (Memory II) to be stored, added, or subtracted as with the first memory register (Memory I).

Multiplication and Memory

12. $39 \times 6 =$ 234	**17.** $39.87 \times 6 =$ _____
13. $15 \times 8 =$ _____	**18.** $17 \times 86.01 =$ _____
14. $15 \times 3 =$ _____	**19.** $20 \times 135.88 =$ _____
15. $18 \times 5 =$ _____	**20.** $6.20 \times 8.3 =$ _____
16. Memory Total = _____	**21.** Memory Total = _____

22. $52 \times 8 =$ _____	**27.** $81 \times 2 =$ _____
23. $56 \times 9 =$ _____	**28.** $11.6 \times 9 =$ _____
24. $9.8 \times 2 =$ _____	**29.** $5 \times 76 =$ _____
25. $7 \times 9.1 =$ _____	**30.** Memory Total = _____
26. Memory Total = _____	

Division and Memory

31. $70 \div 5 =$ 14.00	**36.** $5,205 \div 25 =$ _____
32. $636 \div 30 =$ _____	**37.** $87,624 \div 39 =$ _____
33. $890 \div 20 =$ _____	**38.** $31,421 \div 190 =$ _____
34. $474 \div 34 =$ _____	**39.** $24,836 \div 71 =$ _____
35. Memory Total = _____	**40.** Memory Total = _____

41. $84 \div 7 =$ _____
42. $584 \div 36 =$ _____
43. $62.50 \div 14 =$ _____
44. $8,539 \div 79 =$ _____
45. Memory Total = _____

Answers

12.	234
13.	
14.	
15.	
16.	
17.	
18.	
19.	
20.	
21.	
22.	
23.	
24.	
25.	
26.	
27.	
28.	
29.	
30.	
31.	14.00
32.	
33.	
34.	
35.	
36.	
37.	
38.	
39.	
40.	
41.	
42.	
43.	
44.	
45.	

Inventory Calculations

BOARDWALK CLOTHING				
INVENTORY				

Department/Shelf _T-shirts/shelf 2_   Date _10/1/--_
Counted by _M. Preston_   Priced by _A. Jones_
Recorded by _C. Durbrow_

Stock No.	Qty.	Description	Unit Price	Inventory Value
T-04		Women's T-shirts		
	14	Size S	18.00	252.00
	15	Size M	18.00	270.00
	12	Size L	18.00	216.00
		Total	**46.**	738.00
T-05		Girl's T-shirts		
	15	Size S	13.75	
	11	Size M	13.75	
	8	Size L	13.75	
		Total	**47.**	
T-06		Men's T-shirts		
	14	Size S	22.50	
	13	Size M	22.50	
	20	Size L	22.50	
	15	Size XL	22.50	
		Total	**48.**	
T-07		Boy's T-shirts		
	12	Size S	15.30	
	16	Size M	15.30	
	17	Size L	15.30	
		Total	**49.**	
		Total Inventory Value	**50.**	

Answers

46. $738.00
47.   _____
48.   _____
49.   _____
50.   _____

➤ **INVENTORY CALCULATIONS**

An Inventory form is used at Boardwalk Clothing to record the number of items the company has in stock on a particular date. The department manager asks you to calculate the inventory value for T-shirts.

To work Problems 46–50:

1. Enter the Unit Price of Stock No. T-04 (18.00) as a constant. (Refer to page 26, if necessary, to review constant multiplication.)
2. Use constant multiplication to multiply the Unit Price by each Quantity (14, 15, 12). Accumulate the Inventory Value of each T-shirt size in Memory I and record each Inventory Value in the spaces provided.
3. Recall Memory I by striking the Memory-Recall (Total) Key and record the Total Inventory Value for Stock No. T-04.
4. Determine if your calculator has a second memory register:
   a. *If it does*, engage it and strike the Memory-Plus Key for Memory II to store the Total Inventory Value for Stock No. T-04.
   b. *If it does not*, continue to Step 5.
5. Repeat Steps 1–4 for Stock Nos. T-05, T-06, and T-07.
6. Determine if your calculator has a second memory register:
   a. *If it does*, strike the Memory-Recall (Total) Key. Record the Total Inventory Value for Shelf 2 at the bottom of the form.
   b. *If it does not*, add the Inventory Value Totals for each Stock No. Record the Total Inventory Value for Shelf 2 at the bottom of the form.

➤ **SKILL BUILDER, TEN-KEY NUMERIC DRILL, AND TECHNIQUE CHECKLIST**

Complete the Skill Builder drills, TKNDrill #2, and the Technique Checklist in the usual manner.

Job 10
Review; Analyzing Progress

LEARNING OBJECTIVES

1. Review multiplication, division, and memory problems using the touch method.
2. Review the Non-Add Key, Decimal Point Key, Add Mode, Alignment of Decimals, Subtotal Key, and Grand Total Key.
3. Increase SAM or decrease EAM to prepare for the Ten-Key Numeric Test (TKNTest).

➤ WARM-UP DRILL: 3, 6, 9, AND DECIMAL POINT KEYS

1. Review your ratings from Jobs 6–9 on the Technique Checklist, page 116.
2. Strive to improve techniques marked with a zero.
3. Work these drill problems in the usual manner.
4. Do not use the Add Mode.

➤ SKILL BUILDER

To improve your technique, speed, and accuracy, complete the following drills:
1. Technique Drills A–F, page 115.
2. Speed Drills A–E, page 114. Record your scores on the Speed Drill Record.
3. Accuracy Drills A–E, page 112.

➤ REVIEW OF JOBS 6–9

Complete Problems 1–39, which review Jobs 6–9.

➤ TEN-KEY NUMERIC DRILL

Complete TKNDrill #2 on page 117 by following the instructions on page 13. If you completed Jobs 1–10 in less than 10 hours, repeat them until you complete 10 hours of practice. Do this before you take the TKNTest so that your scores can be compared with others who have completed 10 hours of practice.

Your teacher will administer the TKNTest.

Warm-Up Drill: 3, 6, 9 and Decimal Point Keys

9.63	6.39	2.35	1.36	3.66
3.99	9.36	1.62	4.98	9.31
6.36	3.69	3.57	6.07	2.69
3.69	6.93	7.98	4.32	6.73
6.93	3.96	1.34	3.09	2.39
9.96	9.63	9.03	9.03	1.64
40.56	39.96	25.89	28.85	26.42

Review of Jobs 6–9

Estimating Answers

	Rounded Factors	Estimated Product	Calculator Product
1. 48 x 79 =			
2. 7.37 x 16.2 =			

Unrounded Product

3. 6.21 x 40.7 = _____

Rounded Product

4. 16.3 x .952 = _____

Unrounded Quotient

5. 85 ÷ 6 = _____

Rounded Quotient

6. 7,083 ÷ 27 = _____

7. 314.01 ÷ 44.52 = _____

8. 22,511 ÷ 436.49 = _____

Constant Multiplication

9. 4,516 x 13 = _____

10. 2,674 x 13 = _____

11. 982 x 13 = _____

Constant Divisors

12. 45.28 ÷ 8.06 = _____

13. 628.40 ÷ 8.06 = _____

14. 745.16 ÷ 8.06 = _____

Chain Division

15. 1,272 ÷ 44 ÷ 9 = _____

16. 570 ÷ 133 ÷ 68 = _____

17. 54.52 ÷ 6 ÷ 2.9 = _____

Multiplication and Memory

18. 63 x 7 = _____

19. 40 x 12 = _____

20. 9.4 x 2 = _____

21. Memory Total = _____

Division and Memory

22. 451 ÷ 23 = _____

23. 1,580 ÷ 7 = _____

24. 931 ÷ 35 = _____

25. Memory Total = _____

Answers

1. _____
2. _____
3. _____
4. _____
5. _____
6. _____
7. _____
8. _____
9. _____
10. _____
11. _____
12. _____
13. _____
14. _____
15. _____
16. _____
17. _____
18. _____
19. _____
20. _____
21. _____
22. _____
23. _____
24. _____
25. _____

Decimal Point Key

26.	27.
4.326	31.28
51.988	9.13
3.052	6.58
.189	7.31
.600	.81
.657	.62
5.129	47.06
9.101	21.79
3.288	4.24

Alignment of Decimals

28.	29.
658.329	42.90
98.79	5.87
−.26	−21.839
4.464	385.162
8.9	5.9
53.114	15.00
−427.96	.08
6.08	86.2

Grand Total Key

30.	
982.22	
−66.33	
51.74	
79.02	
	T
−605.26	
6,375.71	
	T
31.65	
−18.60	
−18.60	
	T
	GT

Averages

31.	32.
352.09	198.37
411.82	69.34
796.70	85.13
84.35	658.72
3.19	8.90
207.67	11.82
581.32	60.59
196.44	93.22

Total a. _____   a. _____
Average b. _____   b. _____

Subtotal Key

33.	34.
7.07	20.79
4.37	76.81
23.00	
16.08	S
6.61	6.85
	5.21
S	9.36
110.47	.53
54.32	707.43
89.03	8.55
T	T

Memory-Plus and Memory-Minus Keys

35.	36.	37.	38.	39.
48.12	54.06	12.48	9.80	
53.79	16.17	3.10	31.82	
6.04	1.89	43.76	24.61	Memory
17.37	92.63	25.32	47.72	Total
2.85	3.84	8.15	65.43	
+	+	+	−	=

Answers

26. _____
27. _____
28. _____
29. _____
30. T _____
  T _____
  T _____
  GT _____
31a. _____
  b. _____
32a. _____
  b. _____
33. S _____
  T _____
34. S _____
  T _____
35. _____
36. _____
37. _____
38. _____
39. _____

TECHNIQUE CHECKLIST

Complete the Technique Checklist on page 116. Compare your technique ratings for Jobs 6–10. Pay special attention to those items marked with a zero in the previous jobs. Did you improve?

ANALYZING PROGRESS

Analyze your Strokes a Minute and Errors a Minute progress by answering the following questions. To answer Questions 1, 2, 4, and 5, analyze your SAM and EAM patterns on the TKNDrill Graphs, page 119.

STROKES A MINUTE (SAM)

1. Was there a steady increase in SAM on every drill from Jobs 6–10?
   Yes___ No___ If No, list some reasons why.

   _____

2. How many SAM did you increase when comparing the TKNDrill in Job 6 with the TKNDrill in Job 10?
   SAM INCREASE _____

3. Did you reach your SAM goal for Job 10 that you set in Job 5?
   Yes___ No___ If No, list some reasons why.

   _____

ERRORS A MINUTE (EAM)

4. Was your EAM less than .33 for:
   Job 6 Yes___ No___   Job 9   Yes___ No___
   Job 7 Yes___ No___   Job 10 Yes___ No___
   Job 8 Yes___ No___

5. In Jobs 6–10, if your EAM was not .33 or less, list some reasons why.

   _____

6. Did you reach your EAM goal for Job 10 that you set in Job 5?
   Yes___ No___ If No, list some reasons why.

   _____

Job 11
Decimals; Fractions; Percents

LEARNING OBJECTIVES
1. Convert fractions and percents to decimals.
2. Calculate a percent of increase or decrease.
3. Calculate markup as a percent of selling price.

WARM-UP DRILL: 3, 5, AND 7 KEYS
Work these drill problems in the usual manner.

EXPRESSING PARTS OF A WHOLE
Decimals, **fractions**, and **percents** are different methods of expressing parts of a whole. The dollar in the illustration is divided into four parts. Each part can be expressed as a decimal (.25), a fraction (1/4), or a percent (25%). The four parts added together make a whole. For example, .25 × 4 = 1.00.

CONVERTING FRACTIONS TO DECIMALS
To find the decimal equivalent of a fraction, divide the **numerator** (upper number in a fraction) by the **denominator** (lower number in a fraction). The most common decimal equivalents of fractions are listed on page 122 of the Appendix.

The calculator can convert any fraction to its decimal equivalent, but a faster method is to memorize the equivalents of common fractions and to use the calculator for the less common fractions only.

To work Problems 1–10:
1. Try to work the problems mentally. If the problem is too difficult, divide the numerator by the denominator on your calculator to get the answer.
2. Round the decimal equivalents to four decimal places.

NAME_____ DATE_____ PERIOD_____ GRADE_____

Warm-Up Drill: 3, 5, and 7 Keys
Do not pause between strokes.

735	577	345	359	145
377	733	753	570	936
535	533	703	763	285
357	333	577	255	798
573	555	355	417	645
757	777	397	383	123
3,334	3,508	3,130	2,747	2,932

Expressing Parts of a Whole

.25	Decimal (25¢)
1/4	Fraction (one quarter)
25/100	Fraction expressed as hundredth (25 of 100 cents)
25%	Percent (25 of 100 percent)

Illus. 11-A
The parts of the dollar bill can be expressed as a decimal, fraction, or percent.

Converting Fractions to Decimals

$$\frac{5}{8} \quad \frac{\text{(Numerator)}}{\text{(Denominator)}} = 8\overline{)5}^{.6250}$$

1. 5/8 = .6250
2. 4/12 = _____
3. 1/8 = _____
4. 7/9 = _____
5. 1/2 = _____
6. 2/3 = _____
7. 3/5 = _____
8. 1/10 = _____
9. 3/4 = _____
10. 2/5 = _____

Answers
1. .6250
2. _____
3. _____
4. _____
5. _____
6. _____
7. _____
8. _____
9. _____
10. _____

Fractions

11. 36 3/4 x 2 = ___73.50___   **17.** 63 5/8 x   7 3/4 = _____

12. 7 2/5 x 12 = _____   **18.** 20.35 x   7 5/8 = _____

13. 43 1/8 x 6 = _____   **19.** 32.76 x   1/8 = _____

14. 79 1/3 x 5 = _____   **20.** 88   x 60 1/12 = _____

15. 9 7/9 x 16 = _____   **21.** 4 4/7 x 5 8/10 = _____

16. 1 6/10 x 54 = _____   **22.** 6 8/11 x 40 3/12 = _____

Converting Percents to Decimals

23.   72% = ___.72___   **29.** 62 3/8% = _____

24.   35% = _____   **30.** 51 2/3% = _____

25.   573% = _____   **31.**   368.7% = _____

26. 24.6% = _____   **32.** 15 1/4% = _____

27.   494% = _____   **33.** 6 5/6% = _____

28. 71.2% = _____   **34.** 80 5/8% = _____

Percents

35.   30% of $800.00 = ___$240.00___

36.   43.5% of $50.00 = _____

37. 16 2/3% of $361.72 = _____

38.   73% of $419.86 = _____

39. 33 1/5% of $739.94 = _____

40.   16% of $368.25 = _____

41.   22% of $532.21 = _____

42.   65% of $939.17 = _____

43.   82% of $224.14 = _____

44.   59% of $624.54 = _____

45. 87 1/6% of $1,193.22 = _____

Answers

11.	73.50
12.	
13.	
14.	
15.	
16.	
17.	
18.	
19.	
20.	
21.	
22.	
23.	.72
24.	
25.	
26.	
27.	
28.	
29.	
30.	
31.	
32.	
33.	
34.	
35.	$240.00
36.	
37.	
38.	
39.	
40.	
41.	
42.	
43.	
44.	
45.	

FRACTIONS

To work Problems 11–22:

1. Use the Decimal Equivalents of Fractions table on page 122 to convert the fraction (3/4) to its decimal equivalent (.75).

2. As you complete the problem, remember to enter the whole number and the decimal equivalent (36.75) into the calculator. Multiply as usual, rounding the answer to two decimal places (73.50).

CONVERTING PERCENTS TO DECIMALS

To change a percent to a decimal, drop the percent sign (%) and move the decimal two places to the left. Examples:

4% = .04	62.9% = .629
357% = 3.57	8 2/5% = 8.4% = .084

To work Problems 23–34, convert the percent to its decimal equivalent (72% = .72). Round answers to four decimal places.

PERCENTS

Base and rate are terms used in percent problems. **Base** is the whole amount ($800.00) which is equal to 100%. **Rate** is a part of the base expressed as a percent (30%).

To work Problems 35–45:

1. These problems involve dollars and cents. For answers involving dollars and cents, round the answers to two decimal places.

2. Locate the Percent Key [24].

3. Enter the base (800) and strike the Multiply Key.

4. Enter the percent as a whole number (30) and strike the Percent Key (240.00).

NAME_____ DATE_____ PERIOD_____ GRADE_____

WHEN TO USE DISPLAY OR DISPLAY-PRINT

Unless otherwise instructed, you will decide when to use the display only and when to use the print feature to work each set of problems. Refer to the Appendix, page 110, for a summary of display and printing features and applications.

EXPENSE COMPARISON

Managers analyze the operating expenses of their businesses each month. The present month's expenses are compared with the previous month's expenses to identify trends. If expenses are increasing by large percentages, the managers will want to determine the causes and avoid further increases.

PERCENT OF INCREASE OR DECREASE

It is often necessary to find the percent of change between two numbers as well as the amount of change. If the base (previous number) is smaller than the present number, there is a **percent of increase**. If the base is larger than the present number, there is a **percent of decrease**. Use the following formula:

$$(-.4312) = -43.12\%$$

Percent of Increase (or Decrease)

Base ($865) ⟌ Amount of Increase (or Decrease) (−$373)

To work Problems 46–55:

1. Follow the **Steps for Calculating Amount and Percent of Increase or Decrease**.
2. When the Present Month's amount is larger than the Previous Month's amount, there will be a percent of increase. When the Present Month's amount is smaller, there will be a percent of decrease.

Expense Comparison

Harold's Hardware				
Item	Previous Month	Present Month	Amount of Inc. or Dec.	Percent of Inc. or Dec.
Advertising	$ 865	$ 492	− 373	**46.** − 43.12
Bad Debts	432	220		**47.**
Delivery Expenses	704	645		**48.**
Depreciation	265	278		**49.**
Heat & Light	659	706		**50.**
Insurance	213	399		**51.**
Rent	878	809		**52.**
Salaries	2,692	2,436		**53.**
Supplies	201	82		**54.**
Taxes	445	596		**55.**

Steps for Calculating Amount and Percent of Increase or Decrease

Operation	Tape	Display
1. Set the Decimal Place Selector at 2.		
2. Enter Present Month's amount (492).		492
3. Strike the Add Key.	492.00 +	492.00
4. Enter Previous Month's amount (865).		865
5. Strike the Subtract Key.	865.00 −	− 373.00
6. Strike the Divide Key.*	− 373.00 ÷	− 373.00
7. Enter Previous Month's amount (865).		865
8. Strike the Percent Key ㉔.	865.00% = − 43.12	− 43.12

*On some calculators, it is necessary to strike the Total Key also.

Answers

46. −43.12%
47. _____
48. _____
49. _____
50. _____
51. _____
52. _____
53. _____
54. _____
55. _____

Markup as a Percent of Selling Price

Selling Price
$100 (100%)

Cost
$70 (70%)

Markup
(Expense and Profit)
$30 (30%)

Answers

56.	32.70%
57.	
58.	
59.	
60.	
61.	

Harold's Hardware				
Item	**Cost**	**Selling Price**	**Amount of Markup**	**Percent of Markup**
5929	$ 83.94	$124.73	40.79	**56.** 32.70
6331	162.70	187.85		**57.**
7458	102.53	140.31		**58.**
7870	64.27	117.91		**59.**
8166	180.78	203.83		**60.**
8260	91.29	114.66		**61.**

MARKUP

The **cost** of a product is the price the merchant pays for the product. The price you pay for that same product in a store is called the **selling price**.

   Markup, which includes the merchant's expenses and profit, is the amount added to the cost to find the selling price. (Cost + Markup = Selling Price.)

   The markup can be expressed as a percent of either the cost or the selling price of an item. You will learn how to calculate markup expressed as a percent of selling price.

MARKUP AS A PERCENT OF SELLING PRICE

To work Problems 56–61:
  1. Subtract the Cost (83.94) from the Selling Price (124.73) to calculate the Amount of Markup (40.79).
  2. Divide the Amount of Markup (from Step 1) by the Selling Price and strike the Percent Key to get the Percent of Markup (32.70%).

SKILL BUILDER AND TEN-KEY NUMERIC DRILL

  1. Complete Technique Drills A–F, page 115.
  2. Complete TKNDrill #1 on page 13 in the usual manner. If you made:
     a. .33 EAM or fewer, complete Speed Drills A–E, page 114. Record your scores on the Speed Drill Record.
     b. more than .33 EAM, complete Accuracy Drills A–E, page 112.

TECHNIQUE CHECKLIST

Complete the Technique Checklist on page 116.

Job 12
Multiple Operations

NAME_____ DATE_____ PERIOD_____ GRADE_____

LEARNING OBJECTIVES
Use multiple operations to solve business problems.

WARM-UP DRILL: 1, 5, AND 9 KEYS
Work these drill problems in the usual manner.

MULTIPLE OPERATIONS
Multiple operations is the process used to solve problems involving two or more arithmetical operations.

ADDITION AND MULTIPLICATION
To work Problems 1–6:
1. Enter the addends (34 + 19 + 35) and strike the Total Key.
2. Record the total below the problem (88).
3. Strike the Multiply Key and enter the multiplier (8).
4. Strike the Equals Key (704).

ADDITION AND DIVISION
To work Problems 7–12:
1. Enter the addends (54 + 11 + 36) and strike the Total Key.
2. Record the total below the problem (101).
3. Strike the Divide Key and enter the divisor (9).
4. Strike the Equals Key (11.22).

Warm-Up Drill: 1, 5, and 9 Keys
Keep your eyes on the problem in the book.

159	591	199	571	519
595	115	851	155	441
519	955	499	209	506
995	959	605	599	981
191	911	132	815	275
559	959	599	933	591
3,018	4,490	2,885	3,282	3,313

Addition and Multiplication

1.
```
   34
   19
   35
   88  x 8 =   704
```

2.
```
  936
  852
   70
      x 36 =
```

3.
```
  489
  551
  376
      x 11 =
```

4.
```
  5.31
  9.60
 12.27
  8.45
      x 21 =
```

5.
```
 24.38
 61.88
 72.98
  3.10
      x 40 =
```

6.
```
 216.38
 314.07
  12.94
   2.65
      x 9% =
```

Addition and Division

7.
```
   54
   11
   36
  101  ÷ 9 =   11.22
```

8.
```
  354
  378
  601
      ÷ 57 =
```

9.
```
  414
  935
  627
      ÷ 31 =
```

10.
```
 37.45
 42.60
 81.59
 78.91
      ÷ 18 =
```

11.
```
  3.25
  6.08
   .87
 54.76
      ÷ 15.20 =
```

12.
```
  67.91
 482.63
 149.23
  45.67
      ÷ 19.80 =
```

Answers
1. 704
2. _____
3. _____
4. _____
5. _____
6. _____
7. 11.22
8. _____
9. _____
10. _____
11. _____
12. _____

Commissions

<table>
<tr><th colspan="11">Payroll Department
Bicycle City
Sales Commissions
For the Month Ending May 31, ----</th></tr>
<tr><td rowspan="2">Sales Rep.</td><td rowspan="2">No.</td><td colspan="5">Weekly Sales</td><td rowspan="2">Total Sales</td><td rowspan="2">Com. Rate</td><td rowspan="2">Gross Pay</td></tr>
<tr><td>1–5</td><td>8–12</td><td>15–19</td><td>22–26</td><td>29–31</td></tr>
<tr><td>Rowe, T.</td><td>1</td><td>1,738</td><td>3,531</td><td>3,097</td><td>2,651</td><td>2,149</td><td>13,166</td><td>5%</td><td>13.   658.30</td></tr>
<tr><td>Daniel, A.</td><td>6</td><td>2,031</td><td>3,416</td><td>1,987</td><td>2,522</td><td>2,763</td><td></td><td>5%</td><td>14.</td></tr>
<tr><td>Flores, J.</td><td>9</td><td>5,206</td><td>2,940</td><td>3,856</td><td>4,029</td><td>3,234</td><td></td><td>5%</td><td>15.</td></tr>
<tr><td>Mason, Z.</td><td>16</td><td>5,485</td><td>3,861</td><td>4,023</td><td>5,087</td><td>4,860</td><td></td><td>5%</td><td>16.</td></tr>
<tr><td>Talley, A.</td><td>17</td><td>4,011</td><td>6,529</td><td>5,916</td><td>3,745</td><td>4,223</td><td></td><td>5%</td><td>17.</td></tr>
<tr><td>Lee, H.</td><td>20</td><td>8,820</td><td>6,017</td><td>5,701</td><td>3,229</td><td>7,605</td><td></td><td>5%</td><td>18.</td></tr>
</table>

Addition, Subtraction, and Multiplication

19.
```
    892
   −364
   −109
    586
  1,005  x 27 =        27,135
```

20.
```
    265
    398
   −450
    −26
          x 85 =
```

21.
```
   98.79
    5.42
  −40.81
    3.16
   −4.07
   63.31
          x 14.20 =
```

22.
```
   59.71
  426.35
 −118.09
  316.52
  −65.87
  120.79
          x 24.48 =
```

Answers

13. $658.30
14. _____
15. _____
16. _____
17. _____
18. _____
19.   27,135
20. _____
21. _____
22. _____

COMMISSIONS

The Sales Commission form involves multiple operations.

To work Problems 13–18:

1. Add the Commission Rate (.05) to the memory register. Do not use the Percent Key to do this.
2. Add each row (across the form) to calculate each Sales Representative's Total Sales and strike the Total Key (13,166).
3. Strike the Multiply Key, then strike the Memory-Recall (Total) Key* to recall the Commission Rate. (Do not strike the Memory-Recall/Clear Key [19].)
4. Strike the Equals Key and record the Gross Pay (658.30). Be sure to clear the operating register (but not the memory register) after calculating each Sales Representative's Gross Pay.

*The name of the key that will recall, but not clear, the memory will vary on some calculators.

ADDITION, SUBTRACTION, AND MULTIPLICATION

To work Problems 19–22:

1. Add or subtract the numbers in each problem (892 – 364 – 109 + 586). Strike the Total Key.
2. Record the total below the problem (1,005).
3. Strike the Multiply Key and enter the multiplier (27).
4. Strike the Equals Key (27,135).

ADDITION, SUBTRACTION, AND DIVISION

To work Problems 23–25:

1. Add or subtract the numbers in each problem (526 – 57 + 419 – 255). Strike the Total Key.
2. Record the total below the problem (633).
3. Strike the Divide Key and enter the divisor (38).
4. Strike the Equals Key (16.66).

DIVISION AND MULTIPLICATION

The unit of measure for the selling price of some merchandise ($4.64 per foot) is often larger than the unit of measure for the quantity bought (5 inches of wire). When this occurs, it is necessary to make the unit of measure identical for both items: 5 inches ÷ 12 (12 inches in one foot) = .42 feet of wire. Refer to the chart showing **Units of Measure** to determine the units of measure for Problems 26–36.

1. Divide the quantity by the unit of measure stated for the price (5 ÷ 12 = .42).
2. Multiply by the price (.42 × 4.64 = 1.95).

Addition, Subtraction, and Division

23.	24.	25.
526	920	7,034
−57	−374	20
419	34	−2,314
−255	−178	−487
633 ÷ 38 = 16.66	_____ ÷ 30 =	_____ ÷ 78 =

Division and Multiplication

Units of Measure

Foot (ft.)	=	12 inches
Yard (yd.)	=	3 feet
Dozen (doz.)	=	12 units
Gross (gro.)	=	144 units or 12 dozen
Hundred (C)	=	100 units
Thousand (M)	=	1,000 units
Pound (lb.)	=	16 ounces
Hundredweight (CWT)	=	100 pounds

26. 5 in. at $4.64 per ft.   = $1.95

27. 420 units at $9.87 per C   =   _____

28. 78 ft. at $12.25 per yd.   =   _____

29. 750 units at $3.95 per doz.   =   _____

30. 866 units at $3.12 per gro.   =   _____

31. 2,760 units at $20.36 per M   =   _____

32. 42 oz. at $6.34 per lb.   =   _____

33. 416 lbs. at $126.00 per CWT   =   _____

34. 606 units at $5.94 per gro.   =   _____

35. 36 ft. at $60.22 per yd.   =   _____

36. 857 lbs. at $50.03 per CWT   =   _____

Answers

23.	16.66
24.	
25.	
26.	$1.95
27.	
28.	
29.	
30.	
31.	
32.	
33.	
34.	
35.	
36.	

Insurance Cancellation

37. Davis Insurance Company canceled Miss Brayton's car insurance policy after 185 days. Her annual premium was $4,200.

   a. How much was retained by Davis Insurance Company?

   b. How much was refunded to Miss Brayton?

38. Mr. Zelinski insured his house with Railey Insurance Corporation. His annual premium was $2,598. He sold his house and canceled his policy after 260 days.

   a. How much was retained by Railey Insurance Corporation?

   b. How much was refunded to Mr. Zelinski?

39. Miss Powers insured her jewelry with Greyson Insurance Agency. She canceled her policy after 145 days. Her annual premium was $670.

   a. How much was retained by Greyson Insurance Agency?

   b. How much was refunded to Miss Powers?

40. Premium Insurance Company canceled Ms. Okano's insurance policy after 86 days. Her annual premium was $965.

   a. How much was retained by Premium Insurance Company?

   b. How much was refunded to Ms. Okano?

41. Mrs. McIntire purchased renters insurance with Davis Insurance Company. Her annual premium was $252.00. She moved to a new home and cancelled her renters policy after 125 days.

   a. How much was retained by Davis Insurance Company?

   b. How much was refunded to Mrs. McIntire?

Answers

37a.	$2,128.77
b.	$2,071.23
38a.	
b.	
39a.	
b.	
40a.	
b.	
41a.	
b.	

APPLICATION FOR YOUR LIFE | Renters Insurance

In a weak economy, some families rent rather than buy homes. To recover loss by theft, vandalism, or disaster, consider purchasing renters insurance for your personal property.

INSURANCE CANCELLATION

When an insurance policy is canceled, some of the **premium** (money paid by a policyholder to the insurance company) is kept by the insurance company based on the exact number of days the policy was in force. This amount is determined by the annual premium x days in force ÷ 365 days.

To work Problems 37–41:

1. Enter the annual premium into the memory register (4,200).
2. Multiply the annual premium (4,200) by the number of days the policy was in force (185).
3. Divide the product from Step 2 (777,000) by 365 days to calculate the amount retained by the insurance company (2,128.77).
4. Subtract the amount retained by the insurance company from the memory register.
5. Recall the amount in the memory register. This is the amount refunded by the insurance company (2,071.23).

SKILL BUILDER AND TEN-KEY NUMERIC DRILL

1. Complete Technique Drills A–F, page 115.
2. Complete TKNDrill #1 on page 13 in the usual manner. If you made:

   a. .33 EAM or fewer, complete Speed Drills A–E, page 114. Record your scores on the Speed Drill Record.

   b. more than .33 EAM, complete Accuracy Drills A–E, page 112.

TECHNIQUE CHECKLIST

Complete the Technique Checklist on page 116.

NAME_____ DATE_____ PERIOD_____ GRADE_____

LEARNING OBJECTIVE

Use multifactor and negative multiplication to solve business problems.

WARM-UP DRILL: 4, 6, AND 8 KEYS

Work the Warm-Up Drill problems in the usual manner.

MULTIFACTOR MULTIPLICATION

When three or more factors are to be multiplied together, the operation is called **multifactor multiplication**.

Work Problems 1–10 by following the **Steps for Multifactor Multiplication**.

Illus. 13-A
Keep your eyes on the copy.

Warm-Up Drill: 4, 6, and 8 Keys

Strike each key with a rhythmic, bouncy touch.

886	488	431	648	938
464	644	486	941	468
684	846	782	716	147
866	684	648	802	824
648	468	640	364	556
486	688	864	684	864
4,034	3,818	3,851	4,155	3,797

Multifactor Multiplication

Steps for Multifactor Multiplication

Operation	Tape	Display
1. Enter the first factor (7).		7
2. Strike the Multiply Key.	7. x	7
3. Enter the second factor (6).		6
4. Strike the Multiply Key.	6. x	42
5. Enter the third factor (9).		9
6. Strike the Equals Key.	9. = 378 *	378

1.   7 x   6 x   9 = _____ 378
2.   41 x   60 x   140 = _____
3.   402 x   51 x   58 = _____
4.   329 x   24 x   14 = _____
5.   27 x   244 x   76 = _____
6. 28.48 x 16.33 x   75.30 = _____
7. 51.41 x 90.26 x   1.17 = _____
8. 60.78 x   37 x 217.82 = _____
9.   57 x   28 x   84.31 = _____
10.   816 x   4 x 730.92 = _____

Answers

1. _____ 378
2. _____
3. _____
4. _____
5. _____
6. _____
7. _____
8. _____
9. _____
10. _____

Sales Order

Ski Mania, Inc.
1223 Mohawk Dr.
Burlington, VT 05401

Sold To:
Surf & Ski Shop
898 W. Besmer Rd.
Roanoke, VA 24031

Sales Rep. Anthony Teal

Date: 10/1/--
Sales Order No.: 3501
Customer Order No.: P0781
Shipped By: Truck
Terms: 2/10, n/30

Qty.	No. Per Box	Description	Unit Price	Amount
6	12	Turtleneck – Cotton	12.00	**11.** 864.00
5	20	Ski Gloves – Women's	6.10	**12.**
8	8	Sweater – Cotton/Wool	19.80	**13.**
12	15	Goggles – Green Tinted	8.00	**14.**
9	16	Ski Hat – with Tassel	5.06	**15.**
5	24	Socks – Wool	3.46	**16.**
			Total	**17.**

Invoice

SPH Scrapbooking
4966 Avenue Q
Dallas, TX 79322

Sold To:
Story's Scrapbooking
1207 Galloway Drive
San Antonio, TX 88315

Date: 6/20/--
Sales Order No.: 2610
Shipped By: Truck
Terms: 1/10, n/30

Qty.	No. Per Box	Description	Unit Price	Amount
2	3	Three–ring Album	16.24	**18.** 97.44
10	10	12" x 12" Punch–out Embellishment	5.16	**19.**
15	14	3D Felt Daisies	1.50	**20.**
25	15	1" Glitter Numbers and Symbol Stickers	1.25	**21.**
19	17	5" x 7" Holiday Paper	2.31	**22.**
6	12	Birthday Scrapbooking Page Kit	3.76	**23.**
			Total	**24.**

Answers

11.	$864.00
12.	
13.	
14.	
15.	
16.	
17.	
18.	$97.44
19.	
20.	
21.	
22.	
23.	
24.	

SALES ORDER

A **sales order** is a form describing goods ordered by a customer. It includes the customer's name and address, the date and shipment terms, and the quantity and unit prices of the goods. It is usually completed by a sales representative at the customer's place of business.

To work Problems 11–17:
1. Calculate the Amount for each item using multi-factor multiplication ($6 \times 12 \times 12.00 = 864.00$). Accumulate the Amounts in the memory.
2. Recall the memory and record the Total.

INVOICE

An **invoice** is a statement sent to the customer along with the goods ordered. It describes the goods ordered and their total prices.

To work Problems 18–24:
1. Calculate the Amount for each item using multi-factor multiplication. Accumulate the Amounts in the memory.
2. Recall the memory and record the Total.

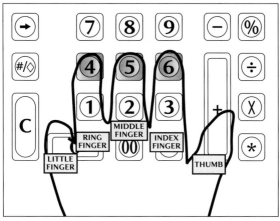

Illus. 13-B
Left-Hand Operation.

NAME_____ DATE_____ PERIOD_____ GRADE_____

NEGATIVE MULTIPLICATION

Negative multiplication is the process of finding the difference between the products of two multiplication problems.

Work Problems 25–30 by following the **Steps for Negative Multiplication**.

Negative Multiplication

Steps for Negative Multiplication

Operation	Tape	Display
1. Enter the 7.		7
2. Strike the Multiply Key.	7. x	7
3. Enter the 8.		8
4. Strike the Equals Key.*	8. = 56.	56
5. Add the product to the memory.	56. M+	M 56
6. Enter the 2.		M 2
7. Strike the Multiply Key.	2. x	M 2
8. Enter the 6.		M 6
9. Strike the Equals Key.**	6. = 12.	M 12
10. Subtract the product from memory.	12. M–	M 12
11. Recall the memory.	44. M*	44

 * If your calculator has a Memory-Plus/Equals Key, strike it for Step 4 and omit Step 5.

** If your calculator has a Memory-Minus/Equals Key, strike it for Step 9 and omit Step 10.

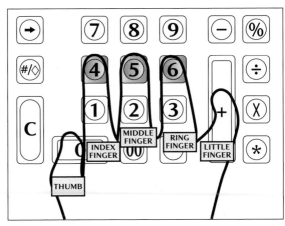

Illus. 13-C
Right-Hand Operation.

Answers

25.	(7 x 8)	– (2 x 6)	=	44	**25.**	44
26.	(138 x 22)	– (305 x 5)	=		**26.**	
27.	(491 x 25)	– (77 x 63)	=		**27.**	
28.	(58.63 x 62.61)	– (149.73 x 32.5)	=		**28.**	
29.	(35.99 x 51.12)	– (48.02 x 2.47)	=		**29.**	
30.	(62.54 x 109.82)	– (58.17 x 49.43)	=		**30.**	

Inventory Extensions

		Selling Price		Cost Price		
						INVENTORY
Qty.	Description	Each	Amount	Each	Amount	Difference
20	Bread Basket	9.22	184.40	8.16	163.20	**31.** 21.20
60	Butter Dish	8.68		5.95		**32.**
56	Canister Set	22.50		15.35		**33.**
38	Cheese Slicer	12.45		5.78		**34.**
117	Dish Towel	6.72		4.81		**35.**
77	Espresso Cup	3.99		2.15		**36.**
26	Frying Pan	13.41		9.22		**37.**
19	Measuring Cup	2.55		1.70		**38.**
70	Mixing Bowl	8.49		5.66		**39.**
83	Potato Peeler	2.36		1.74		**40.**
81	Salt & Pepper Shaker Set	5.25		4.52		**41.**

INVENTORY

Department Kitchen Items   **Date** Oct. 1, ----

Answers

31.	$21.20
32.	
33.	
34.	
35.	
36.	
37.	
38.	
39.	
40.	
41.	

INVENTORY EXTENSIONS

By taking periodic inventories of merchandise available for sale, businesses can analyze the amount of markup on each type of item.

To work Problems 31–41:

1. Multiply the Quantity by the Selling Price (20 × 9.22), and enter the Selling Price Amount into the memory (184.40).
2. Multiply the Quantity* by the Cost Price (20 × 8.16), and subtract the Cost Price Amount from the memory (163.20).
3. Recall the memory to obtain the Difference or markup on the item (21.20).

*If your calculator automatically retains a constant, you will not need to reenter the Quantity before multiplying.

SKILL BUILDER AND TEN-KEY NUMERIC DRILL

1. Complete Technique Drills A–F, page 115.
2. Complete TKNDrill #1 on page 13 in the usual manner. If you made:
   a. .33 EAM or fewer, complete Speed Drills A–E, page 114. Record your scores on the Speed Drill Record.
   b. more than .33 EAM, complete Accuracy Drills A–E, page 112.

TECHNIQUE CHECKLIST

Complete the Technique Checklist on page 116.

Job 14
Production Drill: Auto Repair Orders

LEARNING OBJECTIVE
Process Auto Repair Order forms.

PRODUCTION DRILL
Jobs 14 and 19 are Production Drills that will help you process actual business forms.

You, Robert Olson, are the owner of a small business, Auto Care & Repair. You have one part-time assistant. At the end of each day, you process the Auto Repair forms.

PART A
1. Remove Auto Repair Orders AR-1 to AR-6 on pages 49, 51, and 53; and remove AR-7 to AR-12 on pages 69, 71, and 73.
   a. Leave instructions for Jobs 14 and 19 in place.
   b. Separate the forms at the vertical perforation and cut them horizontally.
   c. Arrange the forms in numerical order.
2. Fan the forms and place them face up on the desk beside your calculator as shown in Illus. 14-A.

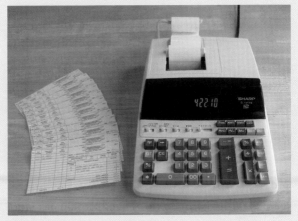

Illus. 14-A
Position the auto repair forms so that you can easily read and flip through them with your free hand.

AUTO CARE & REPAIR — AR-1
2368 Pinegrove St.
Scottsdale, AZ 85251–2368

Qty.	Part Number	Description of Parts	Sale Amount	
4	S1279	H.D. SHOCKS	279	80
2	P0075	TIRE PATCHES		99
		Total Parts	280	79

Name: 7 HORSESHOE RANCH Date 10/6/--
Address: RT. 5 BOX 5661 Phone 555-7955

Make and Model	Year	License	Mileage
CHEV. 1/2 TON PICKUP	1999	CHS-182	57,535

Mechanic's Initials	Description of Labor	Amount	
RO	INSTALL HEAVY DUTY SHOCKS	112	50
JB	REPAIR LEAKS RT. REAR TIRE AND		
	LT. FRONT TIRE	10	00

Comments:
TOTAL LABOR	a.	122	50
TOTAL PARTS	b.	280	79
6.7% TAX ON PARTS	c.	18	81
TOTAL	d.	422	10

AUTO CARE & REPAIR — AR-2
2368 Pinegrove St.
Scottsdale, AZ 85251–2368

Qty.	Part Number	Description of Parts	Sale Amount	
1	B2574	SERPENTINE BELT	58	92
1	T6626	THERMOSTAT	21	05
		Total Parts		

Name: MISS CONNIE DANIELSON Date 10/6/--
Address: 459 STOGNER BLVD. Phone 555-9300

Make and Model	Year	License	Mileage
FORD MUSTANG	2004	GBA-050	69,527

Mechanic's Initials	Description of Labor	Amount	
JB	CHECK COOLING SYSTEM	30	00
JB	REPLACE WORN BELT	37	50
RO	REPLACE THERMOSTAT	52	50

Comments:
TOTAL LABOR	a.		
TOTAL PARTS	b.		
6.7% TAX ON PARTS	c.		
TOTAL	d.		

3. To handle the forms rapidly, raise the top auto repair form with your thumb and hold it between your index and middle fingers, as shown in Illus. 14-B. Use your thumb to turn through the forms.

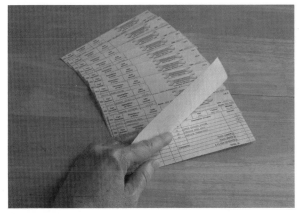

Illus. 14-B

To process the auto repair forms efficiently, hold them between your fingers as shown.

PART B

1. Description of Parts

   a. In the Description of Parts section, add the Sale Amount for each part used and record your answer in the space labeled Total Parts (280.79). The Sale Amount has already been extended to include the quantities (Qty.). Also record the Total Parts amount in the lower right corner of the form.

   b. Enter the Total Parts amount into the memory.

   c. Multiply the Total Parts by the 6.7% sales tax using the Percent Key. Record your answer in the space labeled Tax on Parts (18.81).

   d. Enter the Tax on Parts amount into the memory. (Tax is not charged on labor.)

   e. Clear the register, but not the memory.

2. Description of Labor

   a. In the Description of Labor section, add the Amounts for each labor charge and record your answer in the space labeled Total Labor (122.50).

   b. Enter the Total Labor amount into the memory.

AR-3

Qty.	Part Number	Description of Parts	Sale Amount	
1	C7010	MASTER CYLINDER	193	68
1	S4921	OIL PRESURE		
		SENDER	50	14
1	F8376	BRAKE FLUID	10	90
		Total Parts		

AUTO CARE & REPAIR
2368 Pinegrove St.
Scottsdale, AZ 85251–2368

Name MRS. STANLEY DANIELS   Date 10/7/--
Address 313 PANGBORN RD.   Phone 555-9523

Make and Model	Year	License	Mileage
JEEP CHEROKEE	2002	MLM-128	28,557

Mechanic's Initials	Description of Labor	Amount	
RO	REPLACE MASTER CYLINDER AND		
	BLEED LINES	110	00
JB	CHECK OIL PRESSURE AND REPLACE		
	SENDER	75	00
Comments:	TOTAL LABOR	a.	
	TOTAL PARTS	b.	
	6.7% TAX ON PARTS	c.	
	TOTAL	d.	

AR-4

Qty.	Part Number	Description of Parts	Sale Amount	
1	B7227	BATTERY (STILL		
		UNDER WARRANTY)	50	95
		Total Parts		

AUTO CARE & REPAIR
2368 Pinegrove St.
Scottsdale, AZ 85251–2368

Name PAUL McPHEARSON, M.D.   Date 10/9/--
Address 7504 TOWER RD.   Phone 555-8476

Make and Model	Year	License	Mileage
FORD THUNDERBIRD	1997	SLT-817	27,576

Mechanic's Initials	Description of Labor	Amount	
RO	REPLACE BATTERY, CLEAN AND		
	REPAIR TERMINAL BOLTS	30	00
	INSPECTION STICKER	14	50
Comments:	TOTAL LABOR	a.	
	TOTAL PARTS	b.	
	6.7% TAX ON PARTS	c.	
	TOTAL	d.	

c. Recall the memory total and record your answer in the space labeled Total (422.10).

3. Repeat Part B for each auto repair form. Record your answers in the Answers columns below.

4. Save the auto repair forms. You will use them again in Job 19.

Answers

AR-1	a.	$122.50		AR-7	a.	_____
	b.	$280.79			b.	_____
	c.	$18.81			c.	_____
	d.	$422.10			d.	_____
AR-2	a.	_____		AR-8	a.	_____
	b.	_____			b.	_____
	c.	_____			c.	_____
	d.	_____			d.	_____
AR-3	a.	_____		AR-9	a.	_____
	b.	_____			b.	_____
	c.	_____			c.	_____
	d.	_____			d.	_____
AR-4	a.	_____		AR-10	a.	_____
	b.	_____			b.	_____
	c.	_____			c.	_____
	d.	_____			d.	_____
AR-5	a.	_____		AR-11	a.	_____
	b.	_____			b.	_____
	c.	_____			c.	_____
	d.	_____			d.	_____
AR-6	a.	_____		AR-12	a.	_____
	b.	_____			b.	_____
	c.	_____			c.	_____
	d.	_____			d.	_____

AR-5

AUTO CARE & REPAIR
2368 Pinegrove St.
Scottsdale, AZ 85251–2368

Name SEAN CARMICHAEL II Date 10/10/--
Address 4788 FISK BLVD. Phone 555-4429

Make and Model	Year	License	Mileage
BUICK ROADMASTER	1996	QGA-187	31,012

Qty.	Part Number	Description of Parts	Sale Amount	
1	T9915	STEEL-BELTED		
		RADIAL TIRE	82	15
		Total Parts		

Mechanic's Initials	Description of Labor	Amount	
RO	STATE INSPECTION	14	50
RO	ADJUST LEFT HEADLIGHT	7	50
JB	REPLACE WORN RT. FRONT TIRE	10	00
Comments:	TOTAL LABOR	a.	
	TOTAL PARTS	b.	
	6.7% TAX ON PARTS	c.	
	TOTAL	d.	

AR-6

AUTO CARE & REPAIR
2368 Pinegrove St.
Scottsdale, AZ 85251–2368

Name MR. PRICE DELEON Date 10/10/--
Address 301 WILLIS DR. Phone 555-9144

Make and Model	Year	License	Mileage
FORD F150	2004	T2A-994	129,885

Qty.	Part Number	Description of Parts	Sale Amount	
8	S5729	SPARK PLUGS	71	92
1	F2155	FUEL FILTER	17	80
1	F3284	AIR FILTER	24	34
		Total Parts		

Mechanic's Initials	Description of Labor	Amount	
RO	MINOR TUNE UP	217	50
JB	REPLACE FILTERS	37	50
Comments:	TOTAL LABOR	a.	
	TOTAL PARTS	b.	
	6.7% TAX ON PARTS	c.	
	TOTAL	d.	

Job 15
Review

LEARNING OBJECTIVES

1. Review and improve your ability to convert fractions and percents to decimals.
2. Solve problems involving multiple operations and multifactor and negative multiplication.
3. Increase SAM or decrease EAM to prepare for the Ten-Key Numeric Test (TKNTest).

WARM-UP DRILL: 1, 3, AND 5 KEYS

1. Review your ratings from Jobs 11–13 on the Technique Checklist, page 116.
2. Strive to improve techniques marked with a zero.
3. Work these drill problems in the usual manner.

SKILL BUILDER

To improve your technique, speed, and accuracy, complete the following drills:

1. Technique Drills A–F, page 115.
2. Speed Drills A–E, page 114. Record your scores on the Speed Drill Record.
3. Accuracy Drills A–E, page 112.

REVIEW OF JOBS 11–14

Complete Problems 1–27, which review Jobs 11–14.

NAME_____ DATE_____ PERIOD_____ GRADE_____

Warm-Up Drill: 1, 3, and 5 Keys

315	531	617	911	114
535	351	550	113	372
113	153	835	255	614
351	531	313	330	81
513	513	951	535	733
155	135	553	561	955
1,982	2,214	3,819	2,705	2,869

Answers

1. _____		10. _____
2. _____		11. _____
3. _____		12. _____
4. _____		13. _____
5. _____		14. _____
6. _____		15. _____
7. _____		16. _____
8. _____		17. _____
9. _____		18. _____

Review of Jobs 11–14

Decimals, Fractions, Percents

1. 4/7 = _____
2. 46 2/3% = _____
3. 23.08 x 8 1/4 = _____
4. 72.9% of $2,410.67 = _____

Multifactor Multiplication

5. 9.13 x 15 x 34.89 = _____
6. (6.75 x 8.48) − (37.5 x 28.9) = _____

Multiple Operations

7.
```
    45.69
     7.19
    34.05
     8.31
_____ x 15.4
=
```

8.
```
    738
   − 53
     72
  − 654
_____ ÷ 29.57
=
```

Division and Multiplication

9. 2 in. at $3.43 per ft. = _____
10. 194 units at $11.16 per C = _____
11. 87 ft. at $8.24 per yd. = _____
12. 771 units at $5.06 per doz. = _____
13. 49 oz. at $9.70 per lb. = _____

Multiple Operations

Qty.	Description	Selling Price Each	Selling Price Amount	Cost Price Each	Cost Price Amount	Difference
36	Blender	54.99		27.50		14.
25	Cookbook	23.99		11.90		15.
23	Crockpot	78.99		39.50		16.
54	Grill Pan	41.99		21.50		17.
47	Kitchen Scale	33.99		16.99		18.

Expense Comparison

Item	Previous Month	Present Month	Amount of Inc. or Dec.	Percent of Inc. or Dec.
Delivery Expenses	$ 433	$ 541		19.
Insurance	589	507		20.
Rent	749	800		21.
Salaries	2,521	2,870		22.

Markup as a Percent of Selling Price

Item	Cost	Selling Price	Amount of Markup	Percent of Markup
T83	$63.05	$91.72		23.
B37	41.84	50.89		24.
F20	78.27	85.60		25.
K15	30.76	42.11		26.

Auto Repair Order

Qty.	Part Number	Description of Parts	Sale Amount	
6	S5729	SPARK PLUGS	64	42
1	D3865	VACUUM HOSE	4	74
1	W1039	PLUG WIRE SET	74	80
1	R2001	AIR FILTER	22	40
1	F2155	FUEL FILTER	23	85
		Total Parts		

AUTO CARE & REPAIR
2368 Pinegrove St.
Scottsdale, AZ 85251-2368

AR-13

Name: PAT O'KEEFE Date: 10/12/--
Address: 4511 MESA ST. Phone: 555-6832

Make and Model	Year	License	Mileage
BUICK REGAL	2000	YGN-980	104,877

Mechanic's Initials	Description of Labor	Amount	
RO	TUNE ENGINE	112	50
TO	INSTALL DISTRIBUTOR WIRES		
	AND FILTERS	56	90
		27.	
Comments:	TOTAL LABOR	a.	
	TOTAL PARTS	b.	
	6.7% TAX ON PARTS	c.	
	TOTAL	d.	

Answers

19. _____
20. _____
21. _____
22. _____
23. _____
24. _____
25. _____
26. _____
27a. _____
  b. _____
  c. _____
  d. _____

TEN-KEY NUMERIC DRILL

Complete TKNDrill #1 on page 13.

If you completed Jobs 1–15 in less than 15 hours, repeat them until you complete 15 hours of practice. Do this before you take the TKNTest so that your scores can be compared with others who have completed 15 hours of practice.

Your teacher will administer the TKNTest.

TECHNIQUE CHECKLIST

Complete the Technique Checklist on page 116. Compare your technique ratings for Jobs 11–15. Pay special attention to those items marked with a zero in the previous jobs. Did you improve?

Illus. 15-A
Practice correct posture.

LEARNING OBJECTIVE

Solve interest and trade discount problems.

WARM-UP DRILL: 5, 7, AND 9 KEYS

Work these drill problems in the usual manner.

INTEREST

Interest is a charge for borrowing money and is stated as a percent of the amount borrowed. A formula is used to find the amount of interest charged (see **Formula for Calculating Interest**).

Principal is the amount of the loan (the amount upon which interest is to be calculated).

Rate is the percent of interest charged.

Time is the number of days for which interest is to be charged.

Number of Days in a Year is 360 (instead of 365) because of the ease in calculating. This is called "bankers' time" and is based on 12 months of 30 days each. Use bankers' time whenever the Time is "1 year."

To work Problems 1–8 on page 58:

1. Follow the **Steps for Calculating Interest.**
2. Round the decimal equivalents of fractions to four decimal places and the final answers to two decimal places (refer to the Appendix, page 109, Decimal Rounding Rules).

NAME_____ DATE_____ PERIOD_____ GRADE_____

Warm-Up Drill: 5, 7, and 9 Keys

Do not pause between strokes.

595	779	529	905	725
759	595	507	729	936
975	557	735	915	707
579	795	527	539	549
995	959	774	757	987
759	759	591	257	519
4,662	4,444	3,663	4,102	4,423

Interest

Formula for Calculating Interest

$$\frac{\text{Principal} \times \text{Rate} \times \text{Time}}{\text{Number of Days in a Year}} = \text{Interest}$$

$$\frac{5{,}750 \times 12\% \times 120}{360} = \$230.00$$

Steps for Calculating Interest

Operation	Tape	Display
1. Enter the Principal (5,750).		5,750
2. Strike the Multiply Key.	5,750. x	5,750
3. Enter the Rate (12).		12
4. Strike the Percent Key.	12.% = 690.00*	690.00
5. Strike the Multiply Key.	690. x	690
6. Enter the Time (120).		120
7. Strike the Equals Key.	120. = 82,800.00*	82,800.00
8. Strike the Divide Key.	82,800. ÷	82,800
9. Enter the Number of Days in a Year (360).		360
10. Strike the Equals Key.	360. = 230.00*	230.00

Interest (continued)

Principal	Rate	Time		Interest
1. $4,989	12%	120 days	=	$199.56
2. $3,067	14 3/8%	150 days	=	
3. $6,675	13 1/2%	90 days	=	
4. $4,767	12 1/4%	1 year, 10 days	=	
5. $713	9%	75 days	=	
6. $2,250	12 1/4%	120 days	=	
7. $950	16 3/4%	45 days	=	
8. $497	6 7/8%	277 days	=	

Promissory Notes

Answers

1. $199.56
2. _____
3. _____
4. _____
5. _____
6. _____
7. _____
8. _____
9. $18.85
10. _____

9.

$ 780.00   Fairfield, ME   July 23   ----

Sixty days _____ after this date ___I___ promise to

pay to the order of _____Mike Adams_____

Seven hundred eighty _____ Dollars

Payable at ____Fairfield Savings Bank____

Value received with interest at   14½%

No. 417   Due Sept. 23, ----   *Don Caiter*

10.

$ 360.00   Salem, OR   Aug. 17   ----

Thirty days _____ after this date ___I___ promise to

pay to the order of _____Jill Ramos_____

Three hundred sixty _____ Dollars

Payable at ____Riverview National Bank____

Value received with interest at   11¾%

No. 276   Due Sept. 16, ----   *Gary A. Miller*

PROMISSORY NOTES

A **promissory note** is a written promise made by one person (the maker) to pay another person (the payee) a specific amount at a specific time in the future. The interest rate is written on the note.

To work Problems 9 and 10:

Use the **Formula for Calculating Interest** on page 57 to calculate the amount of interest for each promissory note.

APPLICATION FOR YOUR LIFE
Promissory Notes

Whether you are lending or borrowing money, write the details of repayment in a promissory note.

NAME_____ DATE_____ PERIOD_____ GRADE_____

TRADE DISCOUNTS

A **trade discount** is a percent deducted from the list or catalog price of a product sold to a reseller. A trade discount may be offered to a business to move stock, reward customers that buy in large quantities, or to meet varying market conditions.

The following terms are used when calculating discounts:

Gross Amount is the amount before deducting the discount.

Discount Rate is the percent to be deducted from the gross amount.

Discount is the amount deducted from the gross amount.

Net Amount is the amount after deducting the discount from the gross amount.

To work Problems 11–15:

Multiply the Gross Amount (879.54) by the Discount Rate (13%) to calculate the Discount (114.34). Use the Percent Key.

To work Problems 16–23:

1. Calculate the Amount for each item and accumulate each Amount in the memory.
2. Recall the memory and record the Gross Amount.
3. Multiply the Gross Amount by the 15% Trade Discount.
4. Subtract the Discount from the Gross Amount to calculate the Net Amount.

Trade Discounts

Formula for Calculating Trade Discounts

879.54	Gross Amount	=	100%
x 13%	Discount Rate	=	13%
$114.34	Discount		

	Gross Amount		Discount Rate		Discount
11.	$879.54	less	13%	=	$114.34
12.	$593.61	less	16%	=	
13.	$669.54	less	25%	=	
14.	$75.00	less	45%	=	
15.	$60.00	less	37 1/2%	=	

INVOICE

Cutter's Lawn Equipment
1010 Fall Parkway
Winslow, MA 02726

No.: 198-E
Terms: n/30

Sold To: Anna's Lawn & Garden Center
522 Lenox St.
Ipswich, MA 01938

Date: June 22, ----

Qty.	Description	Unit Price	Amount	
35	Edger—gas powered	89.76	**16.**	3,141.60
109	Rake—plastic	18.05	**17.**	
52	Sprinkler—oscillating	12.50	**18.**	
18	Planter—ceramic	19.99	**19.**	
93	Trowel—wooden handle	3.98	**20.**	
	Gross Amount		**21.**	
	Less 15% Discount		**22.**	
	Net Amount		**23.**	

Answers

11.	$114.34
12.	
13.	
14.	
15.	
16.	$3,141.60
17.	
18.	
19.	
20.	
21.	
22.	
23.	

Net Amounts

Formula for Calculating Net Amounts

100%	Gross Percent		$905.22	Gross Amount	
− 13%	Discount Rate		x 87%	Net Amount Percent	
87%	Net Amount Percent		$787.54	Net Amount	

	Gross Amount		Discount Rate			Net Amount
24.	$905.22	less	13%	=		$787.54
25.	$652.20	less	12 1/2%	=		
26.	$535.64	less	9%	=		
27.	$423.89	less	20%	=		
28.	$307.86	less	18%	=		
29.	$423.99	less	33 1/3%	=		
30.	$721.80	less	42%	=		

Discounts and Net Amounts

$905.22	Gross Amount	=	100%	
−117.68	Discount	=	13%	
$787.54	Net Amount	=	87%	

	Gross Amount		Discount Rate			Discount	Net Amount
31.	$905.22	less	13%	=	a.	$117.68	b. $787.54
32.	$423.00	less	12 1/2%	=	a.		b.
33.	$980.50	less	22%	=	a.		b.
34.	$821.10	less	34%	=	a.		b.
35.	$695.50	less	37 1/2%	=	a.		b.
36.	$750.30	less	17%	=	a.		b.
37.	$194.46	less	8%	=	a.		b.

Answers

24.	$787.54
25.	
26.	
27.	
28.	
29.	
30.	
31a.	$117.68
b.	$787.54
32a.	
b.	
33a.	
b.	
34a.	
b.	
35a.	
b.	
36a.	
b.	
37a.	
b.	

NET AMOUNTS

Net Amount is the amount remaining after deducting the discount. **Net Amount Percent** is the difference when the Discount Rate is subtracted from 100% (100% − 13% = 87%).

To work Problems 24–30:

1. Subtract the Discount Rate (13%) from 100% to obtain the Net Amount Percent (87%).
2. Multiply the Gross Amount (905.22) by 87%. Use the Percent Key to calculate the Net Amount (787.54).

DISCOUNTS AND NET AMOUNTS

To work Problems 31–37:

1. Multiply the Gross Amount (905.22) by 13%. Use the Percent Key to calculate the Discount (117.68).
2. Subtract the Discount from the Gross Amount to calculate the Net Amount (787.54).

SKILL BUILDER AND TEN-KEY NUMERIC DRILL

1. Complete Technique Drills A–F, page 115.
2. Complete TKNDrill #2 on page 117 in the usual manner. If you made:
   a. .33 EAM or fewer, complete Speed Drills A–E, page 114. Record your scores on the Speed Drill Record.
   b. more than .33 EAM, complete Accuracy Drills A–E, page 112.

TECHNIQUE CHECKLIST

Complete the Technique Checklist on page 116 in the usual manner.

LEARNING OBJECTIVE
Solve cash and chain discount problems.

WARM-UP DRILL: 2, 4, AND 6 KEYS
Work these drill problems in the usual manner.

CASH DISCOUNTS
A **cash discount** is a percent deducted from the invoice for payment within a specified time. Payment terms are stated on the invoice. If the terms are 2/10, n/30 (as shown on the invoice on this page), the buyer may take a 2% cash discount if the invoice is paid within 10 days of the invoice date. The buyer must pay the full amount of the invoice within 30 days.

Add the discount period (10 days) to the invoice date (December 1) to calculate the last date that the buyer can pay the invoice and still deduct the cash discount (December 11).

Locate the numbered items below on the invoice. This information is used to calculate cash discounts.

1. Terms 2/10, n/30
2. Invoice Date .... December 1
   Last date within
   discount period .... December 11
3. Date Paid .... December 9
   Was the invoice paid within
   the discount period? .... Yes
4. Gross Amount $959.70
5. Amount of Cash Discount $19.19
6. Amount Due $940.51

Warm-Up Drill: 2, 4, and 6 Keys

Concentrate on the location of each key.

426	624	216	434	614
644	426	264	672	582
264	444	474	416	174
642	222	232	252	963
466	666	606	668	426
244	642	484	296	246
2,686	3,024	2,276	2,738	3,005

Cash Discounts

SHIP TO
Photo Express
119 Oakwood Ct.
Newberry, FL 33034

PHOTO SOURCE, INC.
5077 Merrimac Lane
Fort Myers, FL 33901

INVOICE

Invoice No.: 1037

	DATE	SHIP VIA	TERMS
	December 1, ----	Truck	2/10, n/30

Stock No.	Quantity	Description	Unit Price	Amount
701	20	Non-glare glass	6.67	133.40
636	40	8 x 10 Wooden frame	5.09	203.60
812	15	Collage frame	8.28	124.20
945	75	Photo magnet	1.46	109.50
783	60	5 x 7 Mat	2.33	139.80
210	35	Document frame	7.12	249.20

Paid Dec. 9, ----

Thank you! *SL*

Gross Amount	959.70
Cash Discount	19.19
Amount Due	940.51

③ Date Paid   ② Invoice Date   ① Terms   ④ Gross Amount   ⑥ Amount Due

⑤ Cash Discount

Cash Discounts (continued)

Payment terms...............................	2/10, n/30
Invoice date	May 11, ----
Date paid	May 20, ----
Invoice total	$2,352.60
Last date within discount period .... **1.**	May 21
Amount of cash discount, if any........ **2.**	$47.05
Amount due .... **3.**	$2,305.55

Payment terms	2/20, n/30
Invoice date	December 3, ----
Date paid	December 18, ----
Invoice total	$961.05
Last date within discount period .... **4.**	_____
Amount of cash discount, if any........ **5.**	_____
Amount due .... **6.**	_____

Answers

1.	May 21
2.	$47.05
3.	$2,305.55
4.	_____
5.	_____
6.	_____
7.	_____
8.	_____
9.	_____
10.	_____

INVOICE

Pets R Us
927 Kaylor Street
Gary, IN 46402

SHIP TO
Pet Place
4230 Green River Rd.
Evansville, IN 47701

Invoice No.:	10-351
Cust. Order No.:	G-648
7. Date:	July 19, ----
Terms:	2/15, n/30
Ship Via:	Truck

Quantity	Stock No.	Description	Unit Price	Amount
38	#379	Nylon Leash	3.44	130.72
51	#350	Rawhide Bone	1.59	81.09
23	#430	Plastic Water Dish	2.86	65.78
18	#125	Cedar-Filled Dog Bed	17.07	307.26

Gross Amount	**8.**	_____
Discount	**9.**	_____
Amount Due	**10.**	_____

Paid July 30, ---- J.D.

CASH DISCOUNTS (continued)

To work Problems 1–6:
1. Determine the last date within the discount period.
2. Calculate the amount of the discount (if the invoice was paid within the cash discount period) and the amount due:
   a. Multiply the invoice total (2,352.60) by the payment term (2%) to calculate the amount of the cash discount (47.05). Use the Percent Key.
   b. Subtract the amount of the cash discount from the invoice total to calculate the amount due (2,305.55)

To work Problems 7–10:
1. Verify the Amounts on the invoice and accumulate the Amounts in the memory.
2. Calculate the following:
   a. Last date within discount period
   b. Invoice total
   c. Amount of the cash discount
   d. Amount due

If the invoice date is near the end of the month, you may have to consider the number of days in the month to calculate the last date within the discount period. For example:

Terms	Invoice Date	Discount Period	Last Date for Discount
2/10, n/30	September 22	10 days	October 2
2/15, n/45	April 19	15 days	May 4
2/20, n/60	July 17	20 days	August 6

CHAIN DISCOUNTS

A series of two or more trade discounts, called a **chain discount**, may be offered. A chain discount of 10% – 5% means that after 10% has been deducted from the gross amount, 5% more is deducted from the remaining amount.

CHAIN DISCOUNTS WITH A TABLE

A table of chain discount net equivalents of the most common chain discounts is available in the Appendix on page 121. It is usually faster and more accurate to consult a table rather than to individually calculate each discount of the chain.

To work Problems 11–14:

1. From the table on page 121, locate the net equivalent (.675) of the chain discount (25% – 10%).
2. Multiply the Gross Amount (928.17) by the net equivalent (.675) to calculate the Net Amount (626.51).

When calculating discounts, the net amount is usually calculated first and subtracted from the gross amount to obtain the discount.

To work Problems 15–18:

1. Follow the procedure in Steps 1 and 2 above to calculate the Net Amount (1,889.07). Be sure to record your answer next to (b).
2. Subtract the Net Amount from the Gross Amount to calculate the Discount (734.64).

To work Problems 19–26:

1. Calculate the Amounts and accumulate the Amounts in the memory.
2. Calculate the Delivery Charge and add it to the memory.
3. Recall the memory and record the Gross Amount.
4. Locate the net equivalent of the chain discount from the table on page 121.
5. Multiply the Gross Amount by the net equivalent to calculate the Net Amount. Be sure to record your answer next to Number 26.
6. Subtract the Net Amount from the Gross Amount to calculate the Discount.

Chain Discounts With a Table

Gross Amount		Chain Discount	Net Amount
11. $928.17	less	25% – 10% =	$626.51
12. $623.10	less	10% – 2 1/2% =	
13. $225.80	less	20% – 5% =	
14. $937.94	less	30% – 7 1/2% =	

Gross Amount		Chain Discount	Discount	Net Amount
15. $2,623.71	less	20% – 10% =	a. $734.64	b. $1,889.07
16. $6,489.42	less	30% – 10% – 5% =	a.	b.
17. $598.00	less	12 1/2% – 5% =	a.	b.
18. $757.39	less	30% – 10% =	a.	b.

Tremont Tennis Equipment
22 Ridgetop Drive
Garrison, CO 81230

INVOICE

Invoice No.: 228
Cust. Order No.: 101153

Sold To: What A Racket!
601 Suncrest Ave.
Durango, CO 81301

Date: September 8, ----
Terms: n/30
Ship Via: B&K Truck

Quantity	Description	Unit Price	Amount	
25	Tennis racket	24.50	**19.**	
73	Tennis balls	3.25	**20.**	
42	Tennis racket cover	5.85	**21.**	
51	Tennis towel	4.61	**22.**	
	B & K Delivery Charge @ .26 x __170__ miles		**23.**	
	Gross Amount		**24.**	
	Less Discount 25% – 10%		**25.**	
	Net Amount		**26.**	

Answers

11.	$626.51
12.	
13.	
14.	
15a.	$734.64
b.	$1,889.07
16a.	
b.	
17a.	
b.	
18a.	
b.	
19.	
20.	
21.	
22.	
23.	
24.	
25.	
26.	

Chain Discounts Without a Table

Gross Amount		Chain Discount		Net Amount
27. $578.31	less	25% – 10%	=	$390.36
28. $354.85	less	20% – 15% – 5%	=	
29. $409.39	less	33 1/4% – 10% – 2 1/2%	=	
30. $757.76	less	66% – 20% – 7 1/2%	=	
31. $845.28	less	30% – 7 1/2%	=	
32. $273.26	less	15% – 10% – 5%	=	

Answers

27.	$390.36
28.	
29.	
30.	
31.	
32.	
33.	
34.	
35.	
36.	
37.	
38.	
39.	
40.	

GAME ENTERTAINMENT
3443 Locust Drive
Carson City, NV 89701

INVOICE

No.: 482
Terms: n/30

Sold To: Ultimate Games and Music
704 Ramble Road
Silver Springs, NV 89429

Date: February 12, ----

Quantity	Description and Stock No.	Unit Price	Amount
18	Video Game #701	12.72	**33.**
59	Video Game #636	25.39	**34.**
15	Video Game #812	30.70	**35.**
75	CD #945	9.98	**36.**
62	DVD #783	10.61	**37.**
		Gross Amount	**38.**
		Less 30% – 10% – 5% Discount	**39.**
		Net Amount	**40.**

CHAIN DISCOUNTS WITHOUT A TABLE

When a table of chain discount net equivalents is not available, or if the chain discount does not appear in the table, you can determine the net amount by multiplying the gross amount by the complement of each discount. A **complement** is the difference between the discount and 100%. For example, the complement of 35% (.35) is .65.

To work Problems 27–32:

Multiply the Gross Amount (578.31) by the complement of the first discount (75%), and multiply the resulting total (433.73) by the complement of the second discount (90%) to calculate the Net Amount (390.36). (Therefore, the operation is 578.31 × 75% × 90% = 390.36). Round the decimal equivalents of fractions to four decimal places and the final answers to two decimal places.

To work Problems 33–40:

1. Calculate the Amount for each item and accumulate each Amount in the memory.
2. Recall the memory and record the Gross Amount.
3. Multiply the Gross Amount by the complement of the first discount and the resulting total by the complements of the remaining discounts to calculate the Net Amount. Be sure to record your answer next to Number 40.
4. Subtract the Net Amount from the Gross Amount to calculate the Discount.

SKILL BUILDER, TEN-KEY NUMERIC DRILL, AND TECHNIQUE CHECKLIST

Complete the Skill Builder drills, TKNDrill #2, and the Technique Checklist in the usual manner.

NAME_____ DATE_____ PERIOD_____ GRADE_____

LEARNING OBJECTIVES

1. Understand the relationship of metric measurements to one another.
2. Convert from U.S. equivalents to metric measurements.

WARM-UP DRILL: 1, 5, AND 7 KEYS

Work these drill problems in the usual manner.

METRICS

The metric system of measurement is the standard measurement system used in most countries of the world. Some American businesses have changed from the U.S. measurement system to the metric system so they can compete in international markets. Many items you buy are measured in metric terms, such as 35-millimeter film and 2-liter bottles. The following are several metric measurements that you will use in business:

Metric Base Unit	Type of Measurement	Symbol
meter	length	m
gram	weight	g
liter	capacity	L

METER

Meter is a measure of length. A meter is slightly longer than a yard. Prefixes are added to all metric base units (meter, gram, or liter) to show multiples (more) and submultiples (less) of the base. Since the same prefixes are added to the base words "meter," "gram," and "liter," you should memorize the more common prefixes and their values (See **Prefixes and Their Values**).

Warm-Up Drill: 1, 5, and 7 Keys

Strike each key firmly and quickly.

517	755	525	731	747
751	155	765	537	512
117	717	581	597	137
575	177	507	127	507
715	557	741	741	165
151	771	975	585	781
2,826	3,132	4,094	3,318	2,849

Metrics

Prefixes and Their Values

Less
- deci = tenth
- centi = hundredth
- milli = thousandth

More
- deka = ten
- hecto = hundred
- kilo = thousand

Submultiples of the Meter

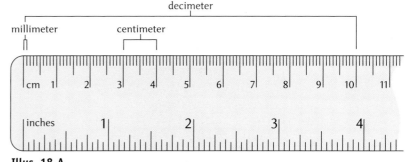

Illus. 18-A
Three common submultiples of the meter are shown on a ruler.

Multiples and Submultiples of the Metric Base Unit

	Measurement	Symbol		Meter	
Submultiples of base unit	1 millimeter	mm	=	0.001	(one-thousandth meter)
	1 centimeter	cm	=	0.01	(one-hundredth meter)
	1 decimeter	dm	=	0.1	(one-tenth meter)
Base unit	1 meter	m	=	1	(one meter)
Multiples of base unit	1 dekameter	dam	=	10	(ten meters)
	1 hectometer	hm	=	100	(one hundred meters)
	1 kilometer	km	=	1 000	(one thousand meters)

Note that there is a space (but no comma) in 1 000 and there is a "0" before the decimal point in 0.1, 0.01, and 0.001.

Smaller Measurement to Larger Measurement

459 mm $= \dfrac{45.9}{\textbf{1.}}$ cm $= \dfrac{4.59}{\textbf{2.}}$ dm $= \dfrac{0.459}{\textbf{3.}}$ m

438 m $= \dfrac{}{\textbf{4.}}$ dam $= \dfrac{}{\textbf{5.}}$ hm $= \dfrac{}{\textbf{6.}}$ km

791 dm $= \dfrac{}{\textbf{7.}}$ m $= \dfrac{}{\textbf{8.}}$ dam $= \dfrac{}{\textbf{9.}}$ hm

14 m $= \dfrac{}{\textbf{10.}}$ dam $= \dfrac{}{\textbf{11.}}$ hm

800 dm $= \dfrac{}{\textbf{12.}}$ m $= \dfrac{}{\textbf{13.}}$ dam

613 mm $= \dfrac{}{\textbf{14.}}$ cm $= \dfrac{}{\textbf{15.}}$ dm

740 cm $= \dfrac{}{\textbf{16.}}$ dm

30 m $= \dfrac{}{\textbf{17.}}$ km

2 579 dm $= \dfrac{}{\textbf{18.}}$ km

APPLICATION FOR YOUR LIFE | Metrics

Many American companies do business internationally. Understanding the metric system can be beneficial to your business career.

Answers

1. _____ 45.9
2. _____ 4.59
3. _____ 0.459
4. _____
5. _____
6. _____
7. _____
8. _____
9. _____
10. _____
11. _____
12. _____
13. _____
14. _____
15. _____
16. _____
17. _____
18. _____

METER (continued)

A meter can be divided into smaller measurements (submultiples): decimeter, centimeter, and millimeter (See **Submultiples of the Meter** on page 65). Meters can also be multiplied to give larger measurements (multiples): dekameter, hectometer, and kilometer (See **Multiples and Submultiples of the Metric Base Unit** on page 65).

MULTIPLES AND SUBMULTIPLES OF THE BASE UNIT

It is easy to learn the relationships of metric measurements because all multiples and submultiples of the base unit are factors of 10. Because the metric system is a decimal system, each measurement is either 10 times or one-tenth the next measurement. This makes it easy to change values to different measurements. To do so, multiply or divide by 10 as many times as needed to get the desired measurement.

SMALLER MEASUREMENT TO LARGER MEASUREMENT

To change from a smaller metric measurement to a larger one, divide by 10. The easiest way to divide by 10 is to move the decimal point one place to the left.

To work Problems 1–18:

1. Study Problems 1–3 carefully before completing Problems 4–18.

2. Divide by 10 as many times as necessary to change from the smaller measurement to the larger measurement in the problem. Refer to **Multiples and Submultiples of the Metric Base Unit** on page 65 if necessary.

LARGER MEASUREMENT TO SMALLER MEASUREMENT

To change from a larger metric measurement to a smaller one, multiply by 10. The easiest way to multiply by 10 is to move the decimal point one place to the right.

To work Problems 19–36:
1. Study Problems 19–21 carefully before completing Problems 22–36.
2. Multiply by 10 as many times as necessary to change from the larger metric measurement to the smaller metric measurement in the problem. Refer to **Multiples and Submultiples of the Metric Base Unit** on page 65 if necessary.

CONVERTING

When working with business forms, you may need to change a U.S. unit of measure to the equivalent metric unit of measure. By multiplying the U.S. equivalent unit by a conversion factor, the equivalent metric unit can be calculated. Use the following conversion chart to change U.S. equivalent measurements to metric measurements.

U.S. Equivalent Unit		Conversion Factor	Metric Unit	
inches	(in)	2.5	centimeters	(cm)
feet	(ft)	30.0	centimeters	(cm)
yards	(yd)	0.9	meters	(m)
miles	(mi)	1.6	kilometers	(km)

To work Problems 37–50:
1. Enter the U.S. equivalent unit (91).
2. Strike the Multiply Key.
3. Enter the conversion factor (2.5).
4. Strike the Equals Key (227.5).

Larger Measurement to Smaller Measurement

63 km = 630/**19.** hm = 6 300/**20.** dam = 63 000/**21.** m

29 m = ___/**22.** dm = ___/**23.** cm = ___/**24.** mm

8 km = ___/**25.** dam = ___/**26.** m = ___/**27.** dm

58 hm = ___/**28.** dam = ___/**29.** m

17 m = ___/**30.** dm = ___/**31.** cm

6 dam = ___/**32.** dm = ___/**33.** mm

4 hm = ___/**34.** m

37 m = ___/**35.** cm

1 km = ___/**36.** dm

Converting

37. 91 in = __227.5__ cm   **44.** 12 yd = ___ m
38. 567 in = ___ cm   **45.** 760 mi = ___ km
39. 38 ft = ___ cm   **46.** 6 yd = ___ m
40. 72 ft = ___ cm   **47.** 256 in = ___ cm
41. 438 mi = ___ km   **48.** 483 yd = ___ m
42. 630 mi = ___ km   **49.** 52 mi = ___ km
43. 33 yd = ___ m   **50.** 78 ft = ___ cm

Answers
19. 630
20. 6 300
21. 63 000
22. ___
23. ___
24. ___
25. ___
26. ___
27. ___
28. ___
29. ___
30. ___
31. ___
32. ___
33. ___
34. ___
35. ___
36. ___
37. 227.5
38. ___
39. ___
40. ___
41. ___
42. ___
43. ___
44. ___
45. ___
46. ___
47. ___
48. ___
49. ___
50. ___

Purchase Orders

CLOTH CONNECTION
6282 Stratton St.
Lincoln, NE 68504

PURCHASE ORDER

Date: May 19, ----
Order No.: 3290
Terms: Net 30
Ship Via: Truck

Sold To: Fabulous Fabrics
401 Coralfont Circle
Fremont, NE 68025

Qty.	Description	Unit	Unit Price	Amount		
13	Flannel; tartan plaid	m	6.58	**51.**	85.54
36	Seersucker; blue/white stripe	m	5.41	**52.**	
22	Cotton chambray; white	m	4.80	**53.**	
51	Madras; multicolored	m	7.33	**54.**	
				55.	

Purchasing Agent _P. Lewis_

CLOTH CONNECTION
6282 Stratton St.
Lincoln, NE 68504

PURCHASE ORDER

Date: June 4, ----
Order No.: 7912
Terms: Net 30
Ship Via: Express

Sold To: Stitches By the Inches
Alameda Tio Clare, 927
Alphaville Residential 5
Santana de Parnaiba/SP Brazil

Qty.	Description	Unit	Unit Price	Amount	
27	Chamois; navy	m	9.08	**56.**	
34	Linen; natural	m	11.42	**57.**	
45	Silk; black	m	9.92	**58.**	
25	Denim; light	m	7.67	**59.**	
				60.	

Purchasing Agent _P. Lewis_

Answers

51.	$85.54
52.	
53.	
54.	
55.	
56.	
57.	
58.	
59.	
60.	

PURCHASE ORDERS

You work as a purchasing agent for Cloth Connection in Lincoln, Nebraska. One of your duties is to find the current wholesale prices for the items on a purchase order. When you contact the wholesalers, you discover that the prices are now quoted per metric unit.

To work Problems 51–60:

1. Multiply the metric Quantity (13) by the Unit Price (6.58) to find the Amount (85.54). Enter the Amount into the memory.
2. Calculate the Amount for each item and accumulate the Amounts in the memory.
3. Recall the memory and record the total.

SKILL BUILDER AND TEN-KEY NUMERIC DRILL

1. Complete Technique Drills A–F, page 115.
2. Complete TKNDrill #2 on page 117 in the usual manner. If you made:
   a. .33 EAM or fewer, complete Speed Drills A–E, page 114. Record your scores on the Speed Drill Record.
   b. more than .33 EAM, complete Accuracy Drills A–E, page 112.

TECHNIQUE CHECKLIST

Complete the Technique Checklist on page 116.

LEARNING OBJECTIVE

Calculate commission pay using Auto Repair Order forms.

PRODUCTION DRILL

In addition to a fixed salary, your part-time assistant, Jim Brown, earns a **commission** (earnings based on a percentage of the work done). Jim's commission is based on the labor charges.

PART A

To calculate Jim's Amount of Labor and Amount of Commission:

1. Retrieve Auto Repair Orders AR-1 to AR-12 used in Job 14.
   a. Fan the forms and position them beside your calculator as shown in Illus. 19-A and Illus. 19-B on page 71.
   b. To handle the forms rapidly, turn through them as shown in Illus. 19-C on page 73.
2. Jim Brown's labor charges are indicated by the Mechanic's Initials column. Add the Amounts for JB's labor charges on all of the auto repair forms to calculate his Amount of Labor.
3. Record the Amount of Labor in the Answers column on page 73.

Qty.	Part Number	Description of Parts	Sale Amount	
2	A2270	GAL. ANTIFREEZE	29	00
1	T6626	THERMOSTAT		
		AND GASKET	15	40
1	B8069	BLOWER MOTOR	159	59
1	F7787	FUSE		34
		Total Parts		

AUTO CARE & REPAIR — AR-7
2368 Pinegrove St.
Scottsdale, AZ 85251–2368

Name ROXANNE LOCKE   Date 10/13/--
Address 112 DENNY DR.   Phone 555-3610

Make and Model	Year	License	Mileage
NISSAN ALTIMA	2000	JAD-328	41,008

Mechanic's Initials	Description of Labor	Amount	
JB	FLUSH HEATER CORE AND HOSES	67	50
RO	INSTALL HEATER VALVE		
	AND THERMOSTAT	46	25
JB	INSTALL BLOWER MOTOR	66	56
Comments:	TOTAL LABOR	a.	
	TOTAL PARTS	b.	
	6.7% TAX ON PARTS	c.	
	TOTAL	d.	

Qty.	Part Number	Description of Parts	Sale Amount	
1	S9721	REBUILT STARTER	215	54
1	S3239	REAR MAIN SEAL	19	95
6	S5729	SPARK PLUGS	25	44
1	A5631	REBUILT AXLE	99	95
1	F8377	TRANS. FLUID	7	56
		Total Parts		

AUTO CARE & REPAIR — AR-8
2368 Pinegrove St.
Scottsdale, AZ 85251–2368

Name D'ANGELO'S DRY CLEANING   Date 10/14/--
Address 3278 SUNNYVALE ST.   Phone 555-9004

Make and Model	Year	License	Mileage
TOYOTA 4RUNNER	2000	CAK-111	51,798

Mechanic's Initials	Description of Labor	Amount	
JB	CHECK STARTER AND REPLACE	120	00
RO	CHECK TRANSAXLE AND REPLACE		
	REAR MAIN OIL SEAL	225	00
RO	REPLACE AXLE	75	00
Comments:	TOTAL LABOR	a.	
	TOTAL PARTS	b.	
	6.7% TAX ON PARTS	c.	
	TOTAL	d.	

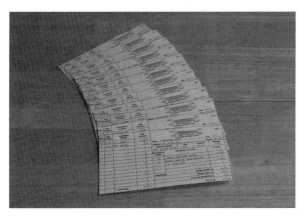

Illus. 19–A

Fan the auto repair forms.

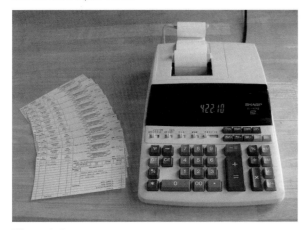

Illus. 19–B

Position the auto repair forms so that you can easily read and flip through them with your free hand.

PART B

1. Jim's commission rate is 49.75%. Multiply Jim's Amount of Labor by the commission rate to calculate his Amount of Commission. Use the Percent Key.
2. Record the Amount of Commission in the Answers column on page 73.

AUTO CARE & REPAIR — AR-9
2368 Pinegrove St.
Scottsdale, AZ 85251–2368

Name JERRY ST.CLAIR   Date 10/15/--
Address 2939 BATES   Phone 555-1004

Qty.	Part Number	Description of Parts	Sale Amount	
1	P2583	WATER PUMP	109	74
1	V8461	HEATER VALVE	59	21
2	R2770	GAL. ANTIFREEZE	29	00
1	T4953	THERMOSTAT		
		AND GASKET	307	57
2	O8125	QTS.OIL	3	73
	Total Parts			

Make and Model	Year	License	Mileage
FORD EXPLORER	1998	PWB-493	80,988

Mechanic's Initials	Description of Labor	Amount	
RO	CLEAN AND REPAIR RADIATOR	65	00
JB	REPLACE WATER PUMP	150	00
JB	REPLACE THERMOSTAT AND		
	HEATER VALVE	198	75
Comments:	TOTAL LABOR	a.	
	TOTAL PARTS	b.	
	6.7% TAX ON PARTS	c.	
	TOTAL	d.	

AUTO CARE & REPAIR — AR-10
2368 Pinegrove St.
Scottsdale, AZ 85251–2368

Name JANICE G. MACK   Date 10/15/--
Address 9237 MESQUITE DR.   Phone 555-1516

Qty.	Part Number	Description of Parts	Sale Amount	
6	S5729	SPARK PLUGS	53	94
1	F2155	FUEL FILTER	25	78
1	F3284	AIR FILTER	23	46
	Total Parts			

Make and Model	Year	License	Mileage
BUICK PARK AVENUE	2003	MET-230	115,422

Mechanic's Initials	Description of Labor	Amount	
RO	MINOR TUNE UP	112	50
JB	CHECK BELT TENSIONER BEARING	21	00
Comments:	TOTAL LABOR	a.	
	TOTAL PARTS	b.	
	6.7% TAX ON PARTS	c.	
	TOTAL	d.	

NAME_____ DATE_____ PERIOD_____ GRADE_____

Illus. 19–C
Raise the auto repair forms with your thumb and hold them between your index and middle fingers. Some operators use a rubber thumb or special lotion to make it easier to turn through stacks of business forms.

Answers

Labor   **1.** _____

Commission   **2.** _____

APPLICATION FOR YOUR LIFE
Auto Care

The Auto Repair Orders show how expensive it is to repair cars. Avoid costly repairs by driving carefully and servicing your car regularly.

Qty.	Part Number	Description of Parts	Sale Amount	
1	H0171	HEAD & GASKET SET	169	06
1	F0232	OIL FILTER	8	94
5	O8125	QTS. OIL	15	96
1	A2770	GAL. ANTIFREEZE	14	50
1	H7039	WATER PUMP	102	74

AUTO CARE & REPAIR   **AR-11**
2368 Pinegrove St.
Scottsdale, AZ 85251-2368

Name ROUTE 54 RESTAURANT   **Date** 10/16/--
Address RT. 54 & HWY. 7   **Phone** 555-4881

Make and Model	Year	License	Mileage
JEEP CHEROKEE	1994	SGP-799	63,209

Mechanic's Initials	Description of Labor	Amount	
RO	PRESSURE TEST COOLING SYSTEM		
	FOR LEAKS	791	00
JB	MACHINE SHOP CHARGES	581	50

Comments:
TOTAL LABOR a.
TOTAL PARTS b.
6.7% TAX ON PARTS c.
Total Parts   **TOTAL** d.

Qty.	Part Number	Description of Parts	Sale Amount	
1	G6961	TRANS. GEAR	67	87
1	S8553	OUTPUT SHAFT	118	79
1	G2837	GASKET SET	7	81
1	G3881	GASKET SET	6	23
1	W6298	WASHER SET	29	83
1	G1567	TRANS. GEAR	48	84
1	G5663	TRANS. GEAR	40	93
1	H9530	TRANS. HOUSING	187	50
1	P6161	LOCKING PIN SET	24	78
4	F8377	QTS. TRANS. FLUID	36	30

AUTO CARE & REPAIR   **AR-12**
2368 Pinegrove St.
Scottsdale, AZ 85251-2368

Name BRIAN DELGADO   **Date** 10/17/--
Address 716 POWELL RD.   **Phone** 555-9877

Make and Model	Year	License	Mileage
CHEV. CAMARO	1993	TAM-541	77,309

Mechanic's Initials	Description of Labor	Amount	
JB	CLEAN AND INSPECT TRANSMISSION		
	REPLACE PARTS AS NEEDED	520	00

Comments:
TOTAL LABOR a.
TOTAL PARTS b.
6.7% TAX ON PARTS c.
Total Parts   **TOTAL** d.

LEARNING OBJECTIVES

1. Review and improve your ability to solve problems involving interest, trade discounts, cash and chain discounts, and metric measurements.
2. Increase SAM or decrease EAM to prepare for the Ten-Key Numeric Test (TKNTest).

WARM-UP DRILL: 3, 5, AND 9 KEYS

1. Review your ratings from Jobs 16–18 on the Technique Checklist, page 116.
2. Strive to improve techniques marked with a zero.
3. Work these drill problems in the usual manner.

SKILL BUILDER

To improve your technique, speed, and accuracy, complete the following drills:

1. Technique Drills A–F, page 115.
2. Speed Drills A–E, page 114. Record your scores on the Speed Drill Record.
3. Accuracy Drills A–E, page 112.

REVIEW OF JOBS 16–19

Complete Problems 1–25, which review Jobs 16–19.

Illus. 20-A
Curve your fingers over the home-row keys.

NAME_____ DATE_____ PERIOD_____ GRADE_____

Warm-Up Drill: 3, 5, and 9 Keys

593	355	531	985	394
359	935	937	392	358
935	593	354	569	795
339	555	957	343	589
593	333	323	563	312
395	999	585	903	968
3,214	3,770	3,687	3,755	3,416

Review of Jobs 16–19

Interest

	Principal	Rate	Time		Interest
1.	$3,870	10 1/2%	257 days	=	_____

Discounts and Net Amounts

	Gross Amount		Discount Rate		Discount
2.	$431.82	less	25%	=	_____

	Gross Amount		Discount Rate		Net Amount
3.	$346.05	less	35%	=	_____

	Gross Amount		Discount Rate		Discount		Net Amount
	$783.29	less	12 1/2%	= 4.	_____	5.	_____

Answers

1. _____
2. _____
3. _____
4. _____
5. _____
6. _____
7. _____
8. _____

Cash Discount

PARTY CREATIONS				INVOICE	
862 Wooden Road					
Asheville, NC 28902			Invoice No.:	231	
			Cust. Order No.:	132	
Sold To:	Balloon Mania		Date:	June 5, ----	
	7113 Brookfield Avenue		Terms:	2/15, n/30	
	Greensboro, NC 27402		Ship Via:	UPS	

Qty.	Stock No.	Description	Unit Price	Amount
42	72H	Mylar balloon	5.42	227.64
19	60D	Birthday balloon	2.71	51.49
33	33C	Helium balloon	3.06	100.98

Pd. June 12, ---- PK

Gross Amount	**6.**	_____
Discount	**7.**	_____
Amount Due	**8.**	_____

Chain Discount Without a Table

CELL PHONE DISTRIBUTORS, INC.	INVOICE
2011 Willow Lane	
Columbus, OH 45420	No.: 2397
	Terms: n/30

Sold To: My Cell Accessories
496 Wildwood Drive
Date: February 21, ---- Warren, OH 44482

Quantity	Description	Unit Price	Amount
18	Acrylic phone holder	5.53	**9.**
7	Precut screen protector	6.10	**10.**
9	Earphone mini jack	6.89	**11.**
24	College logo phone case	11.73	**12.**
10	Universal car charger	12.50	**13.**
	Gross Amount		**14.**
	Less 20% – 15% – 5% Discount		**15.**
	Net Amount		**16.**

Answers

9. _____
10. _____
11. _____
12. _____
13. _____
14. _____
15. _____
16. _____
17. _____
18. _____
19. _____
20. _____
21. _____
22. _____
23. _____
24. _____
25. _____

Metrics

539 dm = ———— m = ———— dam
         17.   **18.**

8 543 dm = ———— m = ———— dam = ———— hm
           19.   **20.**   **21.**

9 hm = ———— m = ———— dm = ———— cm
       22.   **23.**   **24.**

4 km = ———— dm
       25.

TEN-KEY NUMERIC DRILL

Complete TKNDrill #2 on page 117 by following the instructions on page 13.

If you completed Jobs 1–20 in less than 20 hours, repeat them until you complete 20 hours of practice. Do this before you take the TKNTest so that your scores can be compared with others who have completed 20 hours of practice.

Your teacher will administer the TKNTest.

TECHNIQUE CHECKLIST

Complete the Technique Checklist on page 116. Compare your technique ratings for Jobs 16–20. Pay special attention to those items marked with a zero in the previous jobs. Did you improve?

REMEMBER TO:

1. Clear your desk of everything except materials needed for this class.
2. Position this book on your desk at an angle so that you can easily read the numbers and write the answers.
3. Strike each key separately.
4. Use a rhythmic touch.
5. Do not pause between strokes.
6. Keep your eyes on the book. Do not look at the keypad.

Job 21
Wage Earnings and Other Income

LEARNING OBJECTIVE
Perform calculations necessary for figuring different types of income.

WAGE EARNINGS
Many employees earn income in the form of **wages**, which means they are paid by **time rate** (employees are paid an hourly rate that is multiplied by the number of hours worked). To keep track of hours worked, each employee has a **time card** (cards that show the number of hours worked and the hourly rate).

Regular time is the number of hours worked in a regular 40-hour week. **Overtime** is the number of hours worked beyond 40 hours a week. Employers usually pay **time and a half** for every hour an employee works over regular time. For example, when calculating overtime wages, multiply the regular hourly rate by 1.5 to calculate the overtime hourly rate.

To work Problem 1:

Read Problem 1. To calculate Sarah's wage earnings for the week, multiply the number of hours worked (40) by the hourly rate (9.25).

To work Problem 2:

1. Add the Regular Hours and record the total in the Hours column.
2. Add the Overtime Hours and record the total in the Hours column.
3. Add the Regular Hours and the Overtime Hours and record the answer in the Total Hours column.
4. Multiply the Regular Hours by the Regular Rate and record the answer in the Earnings column.
5. Multiply the Regular Rate by 1.5 and record the answer in the Overtime Rate column.
6. Multiply the Overtime Hours by the Overtime Rate and record the answer in the Earnings column.
7. Add the Regular Earnings and the Overtime Earnings to calculate the Gross Pay.

To work Problem 3:

Read Problem 3, then calculate John's gross pay based on the above procedure.

NAME_____ DATE_____ PERIOD_____ GRADE_____

Wage Earnings

1. Applied Computers, Inc., is a company that assembles and distributes computers to retail stores. Sarah Powers, an Applied Computers employee, earns $9.25 an hour. She worked 40 hours last week and wants to calculate her wages for the week. How much did Sarah earn? _____

2.

TIME CARD

Name ___Madeline Kopriva___
Soc. Sec. No. ___999-00-5790___
Week Ending ___March 30, ----___

		Morning		Afternoon		Overtime		Hours	
		In	Out	In	Out	In	Out	Reg	OT
M		7:56	11:59	12:58	4:49			8	
TU		7:58	12:00	1:00	5:01	6:00	8:29	8	2 1/2
W		8:01	11:57	12:59	5:03			8	
TH		7:55	12:01	1:03	5:04	6:05	7:31	8	1 1/2
F		8:02	12:02	12:57	5:00			8	
S									

	Hours	Rate	Earnings
Regular		7.50	
Overtime			
Total Hours		Gross Pay	**2.**

3. Applied Computers' employees are paid for a 40-hour week with time and a half for overtime. John Kramer worked 44 hours at $8.00 an hour, regular rate. What is John's gross pay? _____

Answers

1. _____

2. _____

3. _____

Wage Earnings and Deductions

JOHNSON BUILDING & SUPPLY CO.
EMPLOYEE'S TIME RECORD

Month of ___May___

DATE	TIME From	TIME To	HOURS	WORK DESCRIPTION
5-1	12:00	4:00	4.0	Customer Service
5-2	1:00	5:30	4.5	Customer Service
5-3	3:00	7:00	4.0	Set Up Displays
5-7	1:30	4:30	3.0	Deliveries
5-9	9:30	12:30	3.0	Customer Service
5-10	12:45	4:30	3.75	Stockroom
5-11	9:45	3:00	5.25	Customer Service
5-14	11:15	3:45	4.5	Customer Service
5-15	2:00	6:00	4.0	Customer Service
5-17	1:15	5:45	4.5	Deliveries
5-18	2:15	6:30	4.25	Stockroom
5-21	2:30	6:45	4.25	Deliveries
5-22	1:15	5:15	4.0	Customer Service
5-23	12:15	5:00	4.75	Stockroom
5-24	1:00	5:00	4.0	Set Up Displays
5-26	1:30	6:00	4.5	Stockroom
5-27	1:00	3:30	2.5	Deliveries
5-28	1:00	5:15	4.25	Deliveries
5-29	2:00	5:00	3.0	Customer Service
5-30	1:45	6:00	4.25	Customer Service

TOTAL HOURS

4. _____ Total Hours
__8.50__ Wage Rate
5. _____ Gross Pay
6. _____ FICA (7.65%)
7. _____
__48.00__ Income Tax
8. _____ Net Pay

Signature __Josh Thomson__

Date   May 31, ----

Answers

4. _____
5. _____
6. _____
7. _____
8. _____

WAGE EARNINGS AND DEDUCTIONS

Some deductions from earned wages, or gross pay, are required by law. These include federal income taxes and Social Security taxes.

Income tax deductions are based on the employee's income and number of **dependents** (people supported by the income). The employer takes out a certain amount of the employee's wages each pay period.

The Social Security program provides survivor and disability benefits for eligible citizens, as well as old age and medical benefits for elderly citizens. The tax was established by the Federal Insurance Contributions Act (FICA) and is also known as FICA tax. The employee and employer contribute equal percentages (7.65%) of the employee's gross pay for Social Security.

To work Problems 4–8:

1. Add the Hours column on the Time Record to calculate the Total Hours.
2. Multiply the Total Hours by the Wage Rate (8.50 an hour) to calculate Gross Pay.
3. Multiply the Gross Pay by 7.65% to calculate the FICA tax deduction.
4. Subtract the FICA tax deduction from Gross Pay.
5. Subtract the federal income tax (48.00) from the result of Step 4 to calculate Net Pay.
6. Prove your calculations and record your answers in the Answers column.

NAME_____ DATE_____ PERIOD_____ GRADE_____

STRAIGHT COMMISSION

Some companies pay their salespeople a **commission**, which is the money an employee earns for making a sale. When employees' earnings are based only on the sales made, it is called **straight commission**.

A commission based on the quantity sold is calculated by multiplying the amount of commission by the quantity sold.

To work Problems 9–10:

Multiply the Amount of Commission (3.50) by the Quantity Sold (850) to calculate the amount earned (2,975.00).

A commission based on the total value of sales is calculated by multiplying the total value of sales by the rate of commission.

To work Problems 11–12:

Multiply the Rate of Commission (5%) by the Total Value of Sales (16,878.00) to calculate the amount earned (843.90).

SALARY AND COMMISSION

Sometimes salespeople are paid a salary in addition to a commission. The commission is either a percentage of the total amount sold or a percentage of the total amount sold over the amount that the salesperson must sell.

To work Problems 13–14:

1. Multiply the Rate of Commission (5%) by the Total Value of Sales (850,000) to calculate the amount of earned commission (42,500).

2. Add the amount of earned commission (42,500) to the salary (22,000) to calculate the total income (64,500.00).

Straight Commission

9. The Central High School Band sold wrapping paper to raise money for a statewide competition in Columbus, Ohio. The group made $3.50 on every package of wrapping paper sold. If the band sold 850 packages, how much money did it raise? $2,975.00

10. Brad Gatlin, a college student, has a summer job selling magazine subscriptions to earn money for the upcoming school year. Brad is paid a straight commission of $9.25 for every magazine subscription sold. At the end of the summer he had sold 326 subscriptions. What is the total amount he earned for the summer? _____

11. To raise money, the Dallas Jr. League sponsors a Christmas Bazaar every year. The Jr. League charges each vendor a 5% commission based on the total amount of money each vendor makes. This year Laurel Jones sold a total of $16,878.00 worth of Christmas clothing. How much money did Laurel have to pay the Jr. League? $843.90

12. Tiffany Parker works at a snow ski clothing store for a straight commission of 15%. To encourage ski jacket sales, Tiffany's boss told her that she could earn 17 1/2% commission on every ski jacket she sold in March. Tiffany sold 15 jackets with total sales of $2,738.40. How much commission did Tiffany earn on the jackets? _____

Salary and Commission

13. Joy Daniel works for a pharmaceutical company on a salary and commission basis. Ms. Daniel's beginning salary is $22,000 a year. Her commission is 5%. If Ms. Daniel sold $850,000 worth of pharmaceuticals a year, what would be her total income? $64,500.00

14. Pat Abbott works as a travel agent for Voyage Travel, Inc. He is paid a salary of $2,200 a month and a 7% commission. If Pat sold $38,680 worth of cruise vacations, how much did he earn last month? _____

Answers

9. $2,975.00

10. _____

11. $843.90

12. _____

13. $64,500.00

14. _____

Savings Account Interest

SAVINGS ACCOUNTS Quarterly Interest			
Account Balance	Annual Interest Rate	Quarterly Interest Rate	Quarterly Interest
$592.86	5 3/4%	**15.** 1.44	**16.** 8.52
484.97	5 3/8%	**17.**	**18.**
207.34	5%	**19.**	**20.**
638.28	6 1/4%	**21.**	**22.**
761.69	7 1/2%	**23.**	**24.**
820.21	8%	**25.**	**26.**
400.00	5 1/8%	**27.**	**28.**
924.75	6 1/2%	**29.**	**30.**

Stock Dividends

STOCK DIVIDENDS Annual			
Shares Owned	Par Value per Share	Dividend Rate	Total Annual Dividend
55	$40.00	6%, annually	**31.** 132.00
61	24.80	5 1/2%, annually	**32.**
132	15.63	5%, annually	**33.**
200	26.91	7 1/2%, annually	**34.**
34	7.24	5 3/4%, annually	**35.**
81	16.44	8%, annually	**36.**

Answers

15.	1.44%
16.	$8.52
17.	
18.	
19.	
20.	
21.	
22.	
23.	
24.	
25.	
26.	
27.	
28.	
29.	
30.	
31.	$132.00
32.	
33.	
34.	
35.	
36.	

SAVINGS ACCOUNT INTEREST

In addition to earning money from wages, you can earn interest on money deposited with a bank or credit union. The depositor is paid interest because the bank uses the money for making loans. The interest is usually added to the savings account quarterly. The quarterly interest rate is calculated by dividing the annual interest rate by 4. Interest is calculated on the whole-dollar amount of the account balance. The balance is not rounded to the nearest dollar. Instead, the cents portion is dropped from the amount. If the account balance is $354.86, interest is calculated on $354.00.

To work problems 15–30:

1. Divide the Annual Interest Rate (5.75%) by 4 (four quarters in a year) to calculate the Quarterly Interest Rate (1.44%). Use the Decimal Equivalents of Fractions table on page 122 to convert the fraction (3/4) to its decimal equivalent (.75).
2. Drop the cents portion of the Account Balance (592) and multiply by the Quarterly Interest Rate (1.44%) to calculate the Quarterly Interest (8.52).

STOCK DIVIDENDS

You can also earn money by investing in stocks. An investor buys shares of **stock**, or part ownership, in a corporation. The corporation distributes **dividends**, or profits, to the shareholders. The amount of dividends paid is based on the **par value** of the stock (the value of a share of stock before it is issued to the shareholder). Dividends can be distributed annually as a percentage of par value or quarterly as a certain dollar amount per share.

To work Problems 31–36:

1. Multiply the Shares Owned (55) by the Par Value per Share (40) to calculate the total par value (2,200).
2. Multiply the total par value (2,200) by the annual Dividend Rate (6%) to calculate the Total Annual Dividend (132.00).

LEARNING OBJECTIVES

1. Reconcile bank statement and check register balances.
2. Perform calculations involving checking and savings accounts.

BANK STATEMENT RECONCILIATION

You work as an accounting assistant for Enerco Gas. Your responsibilities include **reconciling** (bringing into agreement) the bank's records for Enerco's checking account. Enerco Gas has an **interest-bearing** checking account, which means a percentage of the average daily balance in the account is earned.

Enerco records all checking account transactions in a **check register**, which shows each deposit, each check written, each **draft** (automatic payment), and the **balance** of the checking account (the amount of money currently in the account).

Each month Enerco Gas receives a bank statement showing the activity in its checking account. The bank statement shows each deposit made, each check and draft paid, the bank service charge, the interest earned, and the account balance as of the date of the statement.

Usually the balance on the bank statement is different from the balance in the check register. The difference can be due to service charges, interest earned, **outstanding deposits** (deposits that have been made but not yet processed by the bank), and **outstanding checks** (checks that have been written but have not cleared the bank).

To work Problems 1–3:

1. Reconcile the check register balance and the bank statement balance for the month of March.
2. The information that appears on the bank statement and in the check register is listed at the right. Using the information given, follow the instructions on the left side of the Reconciliation Statement form to calculate the Adjusted Check Register Balance.

Bank Statement Reconciliation

Bank Statement:

Bank statement balance:	$1,406.04
Service charge:	7.00
Interest earned:	46.05

Check Register:

Check register balance:	$1,554.91
Outstanding deposits:	346.55

Outstanding checks and drafts:

No. 226,	$45.97	No. 229,	$26.53
No. 227,	9.34	No. 230,	14.27
No. 228,	12.88	Draft,	49.64

Reconciliation Statement
March 31, ----

Check register balance:	_____	Bank statement balance:	_____
Deduct service charge:	_____	Add outstanding deposits:	_____
Add interest earned:	_____	Deduct outstanding checks and drafts:	_____
			_____
			_____
			_____
			_____
			_____
		Total outstanding checks and drafts:	_____
Adjusted Check Register Balance:	_____	Adjusted Bank Statement Balance:	_____

1. What is the Adjusted Check Register Balance? _____

2. What is the Total Outstanding Checks and Drafts? _____

3. What is the Adjusted Bank Statement Balance? _____

Answers

1. _____

2. _____

3. _____

Bank Statement Reconciliation (continued)

Bank Statement:

Bank statement balance:	$1,075.59
Service charge:	7.50
Interest earned:	52.69

Check Register:

Check register balance:	$1,180.49
Outstanding deposits:	274.36
Outstanding checks and drafts:	

No. 231, $51.82   Draft, $36.89
No. 232,   10.02
No. 233,   25.54

Reconciliation Statement
April 30, ----

Check register balance:	_____	Bank statement balance:	_____
Deduct service charge:	_____	Add outstanding deposits:	_____
Add interest earned:	_____	Deduct outstanding checks and drafts:	_____
			_____
			_____
			_____
		Total outstanding checks and drafts:	_____
Adjusted Check Register Balance:	_____	Adjusted Bank Statement Balance:	_____

4. What is the Adjusted Check Register Balance? _____

5. What is the Total Outstanding Checks and Drafts? _____

6. What is the Adjusted Bank Statement Balance? _____

Answers

4. _____
5. _____
6. _____

BANK STATEMENT RECONCILIATION (continued)

3. Using the information given on page 81, follow the instructions on the right side of the Reconciliation Statement form to calculate the Adjusted Bank Statement Balance.
4. Answer Problems 1–3 on page 81 based on your Reconciliation Statement form calculations.

To work Problems 4–6:

1. Reconcile the check register balance and the bank statement balance for the month of April.
2. Use the information given at left to calculate the Adjusted Check Register Balance.
3. Use the information given at left to calculate the Adjusted Bank Statement Balance.
4. Answer Problems 4–6 based on your Reconciliation Statement form calculations.

APPLICATION FOR YOUR LIFE
Bank Reconciliation

Keep your checking account reconciled to avoid costly overdraft fees or service charges.

CHECK REGISTER

A **checking account** allows a person to make payments from money deposited in a bank. Payments or withdrawals can be made by check, debit card, draft, or ATM (Automated Teller Machine). Each time a payment or a deposit is made, information about the transaction is recorded in a **check register**.

The amount of a payment or withdrawal is *subtracted* from the previous balance in the check register, whereas the amount of a deposit is *added* to the previous balance in the check register. For interest-bearing checking accounts, the bank pays to the account a percentage of the average daily balance in the account. The interest amount is *added* to the previous balance in the check register.

The information in a check register can help you analyze your personal budgets and determine the areas of greatest expense. Necessary adjustments can then be made in your budget.

To work Problems 7–9:

1. Verify the balances in the check register. Subtract the amount of each payment or withdrawal from the balance and add the amount of each deposit to the balance. Draw a line through any incorrect balance and record the correct amount to the right of the incorrect amount.
2. Calculate the total amount spent for each of the following expense categories by adding the amounts of the payments or withdrawals for each type of expense:
   a. Cash
   b. Housing (rent and utilities)
   c. Groceries
   d. Other expenses
3. Add the amounts in the Deposit column to calculate the amount of total deposits.

Check Register

Number or Code	20-- Date	Transaction Description	(−) Payment or Withdrawal	✓	(+) Deposit	Balance
						887.76
250	4/1	Westwood Apts.—Rent	450.00			437.76
DBT	4/3	United Market—Groceries	62.32			375.44
ATM	4/6	Cash	30.00			345.44
D	4/8	Deposit			378.96	724.40
251	4/11	Corner Store—Gas	21.64			702.76
DBT	4/11	United Market—Groceries	24.47			678.29
252	4/14	Quality Cleaners	7.89			670.40
ATM	4/15	Cash	40.00			630.40
253	4/19	Lakeshore Journal	26.40			604.00
DFT	4/20	Bell Telephone Co.	32.16			571.84
D	4/22	Deposit			217.16	789.00
254	4/23	Uncommon Clothes	39.75			749.25
DFT	4/24	Power & Light—Elec.	27.68			721.57
ATM	4/24	Cash	30.00			691.57
255	4/28	Express Charge Card	198.14			493.43
DFT	4/30	Riverside Service Co.—Water	17.59			475.84
256	4/30	Bob's Auto Repair Co.	50.08			435.76
	4/30	Service Charge—April	4.00			431.76
	4/30	Interest—April			29.58	461.34

7. What is the ending balance on April 30? _____

8. What are the total amounts for each expense category?
   a. Cash _____
   b. Housing (rent and utilities)? _____
   c. Groceries _____
   d. Other expenses _____

9. What is the amount of total deposits? _____

Answers

7. _____

8a. _____

b. _____

c. _____

d. _____

9. _____

Savings Account Passbook

Date	Withdrawal	Deposit	Interest	Balance
1/7/--		500.00		500.00
2/15/--		250.00		750.00
3/30/--			13.13	763.13
5/10/--	125.00			638.13
6/12/--		350.00		988.13
6/30/--			17.29	1,005.42
7/18/--	250.00			755.42
9/30/--			13.22	768.64

Answers

10a. _____
b. _____
11a. _____
b. _____
12a. _____
b. _____
13a. _____
b. _____
14a. _____
b. _____

10. Paul's credit union pays interest at an annual rate of 5 3/4%. At the end of the quarter, his balance is $608.54.

a. How much interest will be earned for the quarter? _____

b. Add the interest to the balance. What is Paul's new balance after a withdrawal of $175.00? _____

11. Derek Higgins has a balance of $621.89 in his account at the Teacher's Credit Union. The credit union pays interest at an annual rate of 7 1/4%.

a. What is his new balance after a deposit of $256.00? _____

b. How much interest will he earn in one quarter on his new balance? _____

12. Samantha opened a savings account with $875.00. One week later she deposited $150.00. She earns 6% yearly interest calculated at quarterly intervals.

a. What was her balance after the deposit? _____

b. How much interest did she earn in one quarter on the new balance? _____

13. Jackie Owen earns 5 1/4% yearly on her savings account balance of $733.45.

a. How much interest does she earn in one quarter? _____

b. Add the interest to the balance. What is her new balance after a withdrawal of $250.00? _____

14. Greg's yearly interest is 5 1/2% on a savings amount of $1,225.92.

a. What is his balance after a withdrawal of $350.00? _____

b. How much interest will be earned in one quarter on his new balance? _____

SAVINGS ACCOUNT PASSBOOK

To have money saved in case of an emergency or a large expense in the future, you can put money in a **savings account** at a bank, savings and loan association, or credit union. A savings organization will pay you interest for the use of your money and reinvest it elsewhere. Refer to Job 21 for a review of calculating savings account interest, if necessary.

After each account transaction, the depositor makes an entry into a **savings account passbook** that shows the dates, credits (deposit amounts), withdrawals, interest, and balances.

To work Problems 10–14:

1. Divide the Annual Interest Rate by 4 to calculate the Quarterly Interest Rate. Use the Decimal Equivalents of Fractions table on page 122 to convert a fraction to its decimal equivalent.

2. Drop the cents portion of the account balance and multiply by the Quarterly Interest Rate to calculate the Quarterly Interest.

3. Calculate the new balance after each deposit or withdrawal.

NAME_____ DATE_____ PERIOD_____ GRADE_____

LEARNING OBJECTIVE

Calculate the cost of using credit and borrowing money.

COST OF CREDIT COMPARISON

When you borrow money, the lender charges a rate of interest for the length of time the money is borrowed. Refer to Job 16 to review the formula for calculating interest, if necessary.

Annual Percentage Rate (APR) is the yearly rate that is charged for borrowing money. It is also a way to compare the cost of a loan. **Finance charges** are any additional fees that represent the cost of borrowing money. These charges are added to the original amount of a loan. Examples of finance charges are annual fees and late fees. Some credit card companies require an annual fee of $50 or $100. If a credit card company is not paid on time, you may have to pay a late fee, and your APR could be subject to an increase.

To work Problems 1–7:

Sam is comparing the cost of interest for three credit card companies. He expects his credit card balance at the end of each month will be about $450. What will be the annual and monthly interest amounts for each credit card company?

1. Multiply the principal (450) by the Annual Percentage Rate (16.8%) to calculate the Annual Interest (75.60).
2. Multiply the Annual Interest by the number of days in a month (30).
3. Divide by the number of days in a year (360) to calculate the Monthly Interest (6.30).
4. After working Problems 1–6, answer the Problem 7 question.

To work Problems 8–9:

Using the information given for each problem, calculate the finance charges and account balances.

Cost of Credit Comparison

Credit Card Company	Annual Percentage Rate	Annual Interest	Monthly Interest
National	16.8%	1. 75.60	2. 6.30
Reward	13.3%	3. _____	4. _____
Superior	23.5%	5. _____	6. _____

7. With which credit card company would Sam pay the lowest interest? _____

8. The balance on Jordon's credit card account is $691.
   a. A late fee of $35 was applied. What is the new balance? _____
   b. If the new balance is now subject to a 29.99% APR, what is the monthly interest amount? _____
   c. What is the total amount Jordon owes on his account this month? _____

9. The balance on Maria's credit card account is $289.
   a. She has an annual membership fee of $50. What is the new balance? _____
   b. If the APR is 11.24%, what is the monthly interest amount on the new balance? _____
   c. What is the total amount Maria owes on her account this month? _____

Answers

1. ___$75.60___
2. ___$6.30___
3. _____
4. _____
5. _____
6. _____
7. _____
8a. _____
b. _____
c. _____
9a. _____
b. _____
c. _____

APPLICATION FOR YOUR LIFE | Credit Card Fees

If you must have a credit card, be certain to make each monthly payment on time and for the full amount.

Borrowing Money

10. Mr. Reed needed to buy a new air conditioner for his business. He borrowed $2,500 from the bank with an interest rate of 11 1/2% a year. Mr. Reed repaid the loan in 12 months.
  a. What was the amount of interest Mr. Reed paid? _____
  b. What was the total amount Mr. Reed paid the bank? _____

11. Julie Hammond wanted to take a summer trip to Europe but found she needed $1,800 more than she had. Her bank loaned her the money at 16% interest. Julie repaid the money in 12 months.
  a. How much interest did she pay? _____
  b. What was the total amount Julie paid the bank? _____

12. Dave, a classical guitarist, wanted to buy a 1977 Ramirez guitar for $2,300. His bank loaned him the $2,300 at the rate of 15.4% for a year. Dave repaid the money in 9 months.
  a. What was the amount of interest Dave paid? _____
  b. What was the total amount he paid the bank? _____

13. Emma Holden wanted to start her own business. In addition to her savings, she needed $4,000. Her credit union loaned her the money at 12.3% a year. Emma repaid the loan in 16 months.
  a. How much interest did she pay? _____
  b. What was the total amount Emma paid to the bank? _____

14. Daniel needed a home repair loan to replace his roof and make other repairs. His bank loaned him $17,060 at 14%. Daniel repaid the money in 1 year.
  a. What was the amount of interest Daniel paid? _____
  b. What was the total amount he paid the bank? _____

Installment Buying

15. Jason purchased a car for $3,500 down and $425 a month on an installment plan for 12 months. What was the installment price Jason paid for the car? _____

16. Tiffany Bowde's parents agreed to pay the $225 down payment on the stereo system Tiffany wanted. Tiffany had to pay the $46.95 monthly payments. If she made the payments for 10 months, what was the installment price for the stereo system? _____

17. Mike Porter wanted to purchase a sofa for his new apartment. The sofa was on sale for $726.00. Mike decided to pay $150 down and $56.25 for 12 months. How much did Mike pay for the $726.00 sofa? _____

18. Karen purchased a plasma television for $100 down and $90 a month on an installment plan for 6 months. What was the installment price Karen paid for the television? _____

19. Alan McConnell wanted a laptop computer for college. He used $125 of his graduation money for a down payment. If Alan paid $95.95 for 9 months, how much did he pay for the laptop? _____

Answers

10a. _____
  b. _____
11a. _____
  b. _____
12a. _____
  b. _____
13a. _____
  b. _____
14a. _____
  b. _____
15. _____
16. _____
17. _____
18. _____
19. _____

BORROWING MONEY

To purchase an expensive item such as a car or computer, you may want to borrow money from a bank, loan company, or credit union. To make money, the lender charges interest on the money you borrow.

To work Problems 10–14:

1. Multiply the principal by the rate to calculate the yearly interest.
2. Multiply the yearly interest by the time (use 1 month = 30 days).
3. Divide by the number of days in the year (360) to calculate the interest paid.
4. Add the interest paid to the principal to calculate the total amount paid to the bank.

INSTALLMENT BUYING

Sometimes an item we may wish to purchase is too expensive for us to pay the entire price at the time it is purchased. Most merchants realize this and arrange a plan of purchasing called installment buying. The customer makes a down payment on the item and is allowed to take it home. The customer agrees to pay a finance charge. This charge pays for the extra time and money it costs the merchant to do business on the installment plan.

To work Problems 15–19:

1. Multiply the amount paid each month by the number of monthly payments.
2. Add the total from Step 1 to the down payment to calculate the total amount paid.

Job 24
Stock Transactions

LEARNING OBJECTIVE
Calculate profit or loss on the sale of stocks.

STOCK TRANSACTIONS
Businesses and individuals determine whether their stock transactions have resulted in profits or losses so they can make better-informed decisions in the future.

To work Problems 1–5:

1. Multiply the number of Shares Bought/Sold (386) by the Purchase Price (33 1/4 or 33.25) to calculate the Purchase Price Amount (12,834.50).
2. Add the Commission (28.87) to the Purchase Price Amount to calculate the Total Cost (12,863.37).
3. Multiply the number of Dividends (10) by the amount (.36) to calculate the dividends for one share of stock (3.60). Multiply the dividends for one share of stock by the number of Shares Bought/Sold (386) to calculate the Total Dividends (1,389.60).
4. Multiply the Shares Bought/Sold (386) by the Sale Price (30 1/4 or 30.25) to calculate the Total Sale Price (11,676.50).
5. Subtract the Expenses (22.50) from the Total Sale Price (11,676.50) to calculate the Net Proceeds (11,654.00).
6. Subtract the Total Cost (12,863.37) from the Net Proceeds (11,654.00) to calculate the Profit or Loss on Sale (–1,209.37).
7. Add the Total Dividends (1,389.60) to the Profit or Loss on Sale (–1,209.37) to calculate the Total Profit or Loss (180.23).

NAME_____ DATE_____ PERIOD_____ GRADE_____

Stock Transactions

Shares Bought/Sold	Purchase Price	Commission	Dividends	Sale Price	Expenses
1. 386	33 1/4	$28.87	10@36¢	30 1/4	$22.50
2. 255	25 1/2	50.12	8@19¢	25 1/2	32.10
3. 460	44 3/4	25.09	7@23¢	135 1/4	18.90
4. 350	67 7/8	18.30	9@75¢	60 1/2	35.00
5. 294	38 1/8	36.65	11@49¢	72 3/4	27.55

Answers

1. $180.23
2. _____
3. _____
4. _____
5. _____

Purchase Price Amount	Total Cost	Total Dividends	Total Sale Price	Net Proceeds	Profit or Loss on Sale	Total Profit or Loss
$12,834.50	$12,863.37	$1,389.60	$11,676.50	$11,654.00	$–1,209.37	**1.** $180.23
						2. _____
						3. _____
						4. _____
						5. _____

Stock Transactions (continued)

6. Jennifer Johns owns 870 shares of Adventure Travel Co. preferred stock, par value $80. Par value is the face value of the stock or the amount each share is worth. She also owns 400 shares of common stock. The preferred stock pays a 5 1/2% dividend yearly. The common stock pays $1.25 per share quarterly. How much does Jennifer receive yearly in dividends? $5,828.00

7. Tyler Darden acquired 1,525 shares of Caprock Oil Co. preferred stock, par value $100. He also owns 850 shares of common stock. The preferred stock pays an 8 1/4% yearly dividend. The common stock pays $.86 per share quarterly. How much does Tyler receive yearly in dividends? _____

8. The senior class of Memorial High School owns 75 shares of Centex Corporation preferred stock, par value $110. It also owns 55 shares of Centex Corporation common stock. The preferred stock pays a 12 1/2% dividend yearly. The common stock pays $.72 per share quarterly. How much does the class receive yearly in dividends? _____

9. Find the amount received from the sale of 775 shares of Blue Pool Co. stock. The shares were sold for 84 1/2 each. The commission was $83.25 and the taxes and expenses were $64.95. _____

10. Donna Dixon purchased 250 shares of Evergreen Gardens, Inc., stock for $9,600. The stock paid a quarterly dividend of $.76 per share. After five years, Donna needed cash to pay for her son's education. She sold the stock for $12,075.

a. How much had Donna received in dividends? _____

b. What was her profit from the sale of the stock? _____

Answers

6.	$5,828.00
7.	_____
8.	_____
9.	_____
10a.	_____
b.	_____

Job 24

STOCK TRANSACTIONS (continued)

To work Problems 6–10, read the problem, then complete the steps listed below for each problem.

6. a. Multiply the par value (80) by 5.5% to calculate the dividend per share, preferred stock (4.40).

   b. Multiply the number of shares (870) by the dividend per share (4.40) to calculate the preferred stock dividend (3,828.00).

   c. Multiply 1.25 by 4 to calculate the yearly dividend, common stock (5.00).

   d. Multiply the number of common stock shares (400) by the yearly dividend (5.00) to calculate the common stock dividend (2,000.00).

   e. Add the answers for b and d to calculate the total yearly dividends received (5,828.00).

7. Follow the procedure described in Problem 6 to calculate the total yearly dividends received.

8. Follow the procedure described in Problem 6 to calculate the total yearly dividends received.

9. a. Multiply the number of shares (775) by 84.5 to calculate the proceeds from the sale.

   b. Add the commission (83.25) and the taxes and expenses (64.95) to calculate the sales expenses.

   c. Subtract answer b from a to calculate the amount received from the sale.

10. a. Multiply .76 by 4 to calculate the dividend per share.

    b. Multiply the number of shares (250) by the dividend per share (from Step 10a) to calculate the yearly dividend.

    c. Multiply the yearly dividend (from Step10b) by 5 to calculate the total dividends received.

    d. Subtract the purchase of stock (9,600.00) from the sale of stock (12,075.00) to calculate the profit.

LEARNING OBJECTIVES

1. Review and improve your ability to solve problems involving savings account interest, stock dividends, and bank statement reconciliation.
2. Increase SAM or decrease EAM to prepare for the Ten-Key Numeric Test (TKNTest).

SKILL BUILDER

To improve your technique, speed, and accuracy, complete the following drills:

1. Technique Drills A–F, page 115.
2. Speed Drills A–E, page 114. Record your scores on the Speed Drill Record.
3. Accuracy Drills A–E, page 112.

REVIEW OF JOBS 21–24

Complete Problems 1–25, which review Jobs 21–24.

NAME_____ DATE_____ PERIOD_____ GRADE_____

Review of Jobs 21–24

Savings Account Interest

SAVINGS ACCOUNTS Quarterly Interest			
Account Balance	Annual Interest Rate	Quarterly Interest Rate	Quarterly Interest
$556.70	6%	1. _____	2. _____
756.11	6 1/4%	3. _____	4. _____
282.67	7 1/2%	5. _____	6. _____
450.00	5 3/8%	7. _____	8. _____
948.54	4 5/8%	9. _____	10. _____
912.87	8%	11. _____	12. _____
205.92	6 1/2%	13. _____	14. _____
569.55	5 1/8%	15. _____	16. _____

Stock Dividends

STOCK DIVIDENDS Annual			
Shares Owned	Par Value per Share	Dividend Rate	Total Annual Dividend
90	$11.71	6 1/4%, annually	17. _____
121	7.48	4 1/4%, annually	18. _____
70	10.22	7 1/2%, annually	19. _____
55	25.91	8%, annually	20. _____
116	30.36	5%, annually	21. _____
87	20.61	6 1/2%, annually	22. _____

Answers

1. _____
2. _____
3. _____
4. _____
5. _____
6. _____
7. _____
8. _____
9. _____
10. _____
11. _____
12. _____
13. _____
14. _____
15. _____
16. _____
17. _____
18. _____
19. _____
20. _____
21. _____
22. _____

Bank Statement Reconciliation

Bank Statement:

Bank statement balance:	$1,163.52
Service charge:	7.00
Interest earned:	35.12

Check Register:

Check register balance:	$1,217.78
Outstanding deposits:	254.69
Outstanding checks and drafts:	

No. 468,	$32.68	No. 470,	$14.27
No. 469,	16.33	Draft,	9.22
Draft,	45.99	No. 471,	53.82

Reconciliation Statement
June 30, ----

Check register balance: _____	Bank statement balance: _____
Deduct service charge: _____	Add outstanding deposits: _____
Add interest earned: _____	Deduct outstanding checks and drafts: _____
	_____
	_____
	_____
	_____
	_____
	Total outstanding checks and drafts: _____
Adjusted Check Register Balance: _____	Adjusted Bank Statement Balance: _____

23. What is the Adjusted Check Register Balance? _____

24. What is the Total Outstanding Checks and drafts? _____

25. What is the Adjusted Bank Statement Balance? _____

Answers

23. _____

24. _____

25. _____

TEN-KEY NUMERIC DRILL

Complete TKNDrill #2 on page 117 by following the instructions on page 13.

If you completed Jobs 1–25 in less than 25 hours, repeat them until you complete 25 hours of practice. Do this before you take the TKNTest so that your scores can be compared with others who have completed 25 hours of practice.

Your teacher will administer the TKNTest.

REMEMBER TO:

1. Clear your desk of everything except materials needed for this class.
2. Position this book on your desk at an angle so that you can easily read the numbers and write the answers.
3. Strike each key separately.
4. Use a rhythmic touch.
5. Do not pause between strokes.
6. Keep your eyes on the book. Do not look at the keypad.

Job 26
Controlling Household Expenses

LEARNING OBJECTIVE

Perform calculations involving personal budgeting and finance.

HOUSEHOLD BUDGET

A **budget** is a financial plan that shows how much money you expect to save and spend. Following a well-planned budget can help prevent you from spending more than you earn, giving you financial peace of mind.

To work Problems 1–4:

Brenda wants to know where her money is being spent each month. Calculate Brenda's monthly household budget for each expense category.

1. Add lines e–i in Column A to calculate the Utilities Subtotal. Add the amount to the memory. Record your answer in Column B, Problem 1.
2. Add lines k–n in Column A to calculate the Transportation Subtotal. Add the amount to the memory. Record your answer in Column B, Problem 2.
3. Add lines r–t in Column A to calculate the Health Subtotal. Add the amount to the memory. Record your answer in Column B, Problem 3.
4. Add the amounts for the remaining expense categories in Column B. Add the total to the memory.
5. Recall the memory and record Brenda's Total Monthly Expenses in Column B, Problem 4.

APPLICATION FOR YOUR LIFE
Household Budget

Begin now the important habit of preparing and following a household budget.

Household Budget

HOUSEHOLD BUDGET		
Expense	**Column A**	**Column B**
a. Contributions		200.00
b. Savings		125.00
c. Housing		1,000.00
d. Utilities		
e. Electricity	130.00	
f. Water	90.00	
g. Gas	101.00	
h. Phone	125.00	
i. Cable	120.00	
Utilities Subtotal		**1.** _____
j. Transportation		
k. Car Payment	500.00	
l. Gas	200.00	
m. Repairs	35.00	
n. Insurance	132.00	
Transportation Subtotal		**2.** _____
o. Food		525.00
p. Clothing		120.00
q. Health		
r. Health Insurance	350.00	
s. Medications	30.00	
t. Life Insurance	70.00	
Health Subtotal		**3.** _____
u. Recreation		200.00
v. Miscellaneous		350.00
Total Monthly Expenses		**4.** _____

Answers

1. _____
2. _____
3. _____
4. _____

Household Budget (continued)

MONTHLY BUDGET PERCENTAGES			
Expense Category	**Monthly Total**	**Recommended Percentage**	**Actual Percentage**
Contributions	200.00	5–10%	5. 5%
Savings		5–10%	6.
Housing		25–30%	7.
Utilities		5–10%	8.
Transportation		10–15%	9.
Food		5–15%	10.
Clothing		2–7%	11.
Health		5–10%	12.
Recreation		5–10%	13.
Miscellaneous		5–10%	14.
Total Monthly Expenses			

Answers

5. _____ 5%
6. _____
7. _____
8. _____
9. _____
10. _____
11. _____
12. _____
13. _____
14. _____
15. _____
16. _____
17. _____
18. _____
19. _____

15. Brenda chooses a less expensive telephone, cell phone, and cable package. This decreases her monthly Utilities total by $104. What is the new actual percentage for the Utilities category? _____

16. Brenda refinances her car loan, lowering the car payment by $106; changes the deductible on her car insurance, reducing the insurance payment by $45; and minimizes unnecessary driving, lowering her gas expense by $35. With these reductions, Brenda's monthly Transportation total decreases by $186. What is the new actual percentage for the Transportation category? _____

17. Brenda's landlord increases her monthly rent by $150. What is the new actual percentage for the Housing category? _____

18. Brenda's health insurance premium increases by $30 each month. What is the new actual percentage for the Health category? _____

19. Brenda makes a conscious effort to begin living on less and decides to have a garage sale. The sale makes $266, and she applies the money to her savings. What is the new actual percentage for the Savings category? _____

HOUSEHOLD BUDGET (continued)

Recommended budget percentages are guidelines used to set spending goals for household expenses. Your budget percentages should be within the recommended range for each expense category.

Budget percentages help you determine the amount to spend in each category. If an expense exceeds the recommended range, reduce spending for that expense. If an expense is below the recommended range (for example, Contributions or Savings), consider increasing that amount by reducing other expenses (such as Recreation or Miscellaneous).

To work Problems 5–14:

Brenda wants to know how her budget compares to the recommended budget percentages. This information will help her manage spending. Calculate the budget percentage for each of Brenda's expense categories.

1. Fill in the Monthly Total column for each expense category in the table at left. These amounts are found in Column B of the table on page 91.
2. For each expense category, divide the Monthly Total (200.00) by the Total Monthly Expenses amount (which is also the monthly income) to calculate the Actual Percentage of the total budget (5%). Use constant division. Refer to Job 8, page 30 for a review of constant divisors, if necessary.

To work Problems 15–19:

Brenda wants to change her budget to meet the recommended percentages. Using the information given for each problem, calculate Brenda's new actual percentages.

NAME_____ DATE_____ PERIOD_____ GRADE_____

HOUSING EXPENDITURES

Housing **expenditures** (expenses) are an important consideration when planning a personal budget. Housing expenditures include mortgage loan payments, property taxes, home insurance, and utilities. If renting is preferred, expenditures include rent payments, renters insurance, and possibly utilities. Renting is more common for an apartment than for a house. The following general guidelines are suggested to help plan housing expenditures:

a. The purchase price of a home should not exceed 2 1/2 times the annual **gross income** (income before taxes are deducted).

b. Annual housing expenditures (renting or owning, including taxes, insurance, and utilities) should not exceed 30% of annual gross income.

To work Problems 20–43:

1. Multiply the Qualifying Annual Gross Income (30,000) by 2.5 to calculate the Maximum House Price (75,000). Use constant multiplication. Refer to Job 7, page 26, for a review of constant multiplication, if necessary.

2. Multiply the Qualifying Annual Gross Income (30,000) by 30% to calculate the Maximum Yearly Expenditure (9,000). Use constant multiplication.

3. Divide the Maximum Yearly Expenditure (9,000) by 12 (12 months in a year) to calculate the Maximum Monthly Expenditure (750). Use constant division.

Housing Expenditures

HOUSING EXPENDITURES Qualifying Incomes			
Qualifying Annual Gross Income	Maximum House Price	Maximum Yearly Expenditure	Maximum Monthly Expenditure
$30,000	20. 75,000	21. 9,000	22. 750
40,000	23.	24.	25.
50,000	26.	27.	28.
60,000	29.	30.	31.
70,000	32.	33.	34.
80,000	35.	36.	37.
85,000	38.	39.	40.
90,000	41.	42.	43.

Answers

20.	$75,000
21.	$9,000
22.	$750
23.	
24.	
25.	
26.	
27.	
28.	
29.	
30.	
31.	
32.	
33.	
34.	
35.	
36.	
37.	
38.	
39.	
40.	
41.	
42.	
43.	

Vacation Travel Expenses

TRAVEL EXPENSE REPORT

Name _The Miller Family_
Date _June 19-23_
City _Orlando, Florida_
Purpose _Summer Vacation_

Date	Plane	Ground Trans.	Hotel	Break-fast	Lunch	Dinner	Tips	Miscellaneous Item	Miscellaneous Amt.	Total
6/19	a 1,136.40		151.62	21.00	22.30	30.36	7.20			44. _____
6/20		b 263.76	151.62	18.98	20.60	36.22	5.70	Sea World	100.80	45. _____
6/21			151.62	21.82	20.33	29.68	8.70	Disney World	249.60	46. _____
6/22		c 78.34	151.62	21.48	18.70	50.59	13.20	Busch Gardens	105.36	47. _____
6/23			d	19.60	23.36	39.67	6.60			48. _____
Total	49.	50.	51.	52.	53.	54.	55.		56.	57. _____ Grand Total

Explanation:
a. Plane fare, Indiana–Florida–Indiana
b. Car rental
c. Gas
d. Hotel bill paid in full on 6/23

58. a. Did the Millers overspend or underspend on the trip according to their estimated budget? _____

b. By what amount did they overspend or underspend? _____

Answers

44. _____
45. _____
46. _____
47. _____
48. _____
49. _____
50. _____
51. _____
52. _____
53. _____
54. _____
55. _____
56. _____
57. _____
58a. _____
  b. _____

Job 26

VACATION TRAVEL EXPENSES

Recreation expenses should be considered when planning a personal budget. **Recreation expenses** may include eating out, going to a movie, or vacation costs such as transportation, lodging, meals, and miscellaneous expenses related to the trip.

A Travel Expense Report, or a similar form, that is used in business may be used when planning a personal trip as well.

To work Problems 44–58:

The Miller family used a Travel Expense Report to record the expenses of their summer vacation in Florida.

1. Add the expense amounts across to calculate the Total for each day. Add each total to the memory.
2. Recall the memory to obtain the Grand Total expense for the trip.
3. Add the expense amounts down to calculate the Total for each type of expense. Add each total to the memory.
4. Recall the memory to obtain the Grand Total expense for the trip.
5. If your calculations are correct, the Grand Total amounts calculated in Steps 2 and 4 will be the same. If not, work the problems again beginning with Step 1.
6. When planning their budget, the Millers estimated $3,000 would be spent on the vacation. Calculate the amount overspent or underspent on the trip.

NAME_____ DATE_____ PERIOD_____ GRADE_____

LEARNING OBJECTIVE

Calculate the financing and budget for owning an automobile.

FINANCING AN AUTOMOBILE

Many people take out loans when buying an automobile. Refer to Job 23 for a review of borrowing money, if necessary. The buyer has possession of the vehicle but does not own it until the loan is paid. If the buyer does not make the loan payments when they are due, the lender can **repossess,** or take back, the vehicle. Problems in this job are simplified versions of an auto dealership's calculations.

To work Problems 1–4:

1. Lines a–c: Add the sticker price, sales tax, and title and registration amounts to calculate the Total Cost.
2. Lines d and e: Subtract the cash rebate and down payment amounts to calculate the Remaining Balance.
3. Line f: Add the APR Financing amount to the Remaining Balance to calculate the Net Cost.
4. Line g: Divide the Net Cost by the Loan Time (60) to calculate the Monthly Loan Payment.

To work Problems 5–6:

1. Add the Remaining Balance amount calculated in the table to the new APR financing amount (567.72) to calculate the new net cost (19,260.72).
2. Divide the net cost by the number of months (36) to calculate the new monthly payment (535.02).

APPLICATION FOR YOUR LIFE

Auto Financing

To be an informed consumer, use internet websites with financial calculators and tips for car buying.

Financing an Automobile

MONTHLY AUTO PAYMENT	
Purchase Cost	**Amount**
a. Sticker Price	$19,100.00
b. Sales Tax	1,194.00
c. Title and Registration	324.00
Total Cost **1.** _____	
d. Cash Rebate	1,000.00
e. Down Payment	925.00
Remaining Balance **2.** _____	
f. APR Financing	932.40
Net Cost **3.** _____	
g. Loan Time	60 months
Monthly Loan Payment **4.** _____	

5. The buyer wants to know what her monthly payment will be with different loan times. The APR is 1.9%. What is the new monthly payment for a loan of:

a. 36 months with APR financing of $567.72? ___$535.02___

b. 48 months with APR financing of $749.40? _____

c. 72 months with APR financing of $1,116.36? _____

6. A buyer has a bad credit record so his APR is 18%. Using the same Remaining Balance amount, what is the new monthly payment for a loan of:

a. 36 months with APR financing of $5,818.32? _____

b. 48 months with APR financing of $7,862.04? _____

c. 60 months with APR financing of $10,001.40? _____

d. 72 months with APR financing of $12,233.88? _____

Answers

1. _____
2. _____
3. _____
4. _____
5a. ___$535.02___
b. _____
c. _____
6a. _____
b. _____
c. _____
d. _____

Automobile Expenditures

TOTAL MONTHLY AUTO EXPENSES Estimation		
Ownership Cost	**Monthly Cost**	**Cost per Mile**
A. Fixed Costs:		
Installment loan payment	$347.66	**10.** .35
Auto insurance	89.90	**11.**
License plates/inspection	10.50	**12.**
Total Fixed Costs	**7.**	**13.**
B. Variable Costs:		
Gasoline	$97.68	**14.**
Oil	6.00	**15.**
Tires	9.84	**16.**
Maintenance/repairs	56.17	**17.**
Total Variable Costs	**8.**	**18.**
Total Monthly Ownership Cost	**9.**	**19.**

Answers

7. _____
8. _____
9. _____
10. _____ $.35
11. _____
12. _____
13. _____
14. _____
15. _____
16. _____
17. _____
18. _____
19. _____

AUTOMOBILE EXPENDITURES

Individuals determine the cost of operating an automobile so they can anticipate and control expenses. Automobile expenditures include **fixed costs** (costs that are the same each month) and **variable costs** (costs that change each month). The installment loan payment would be an example of a fixed cost, while the gasoline would be a variable cost. Expenses that occur infrequently, such as tire purchases, are usually divided by 12 (12 months in a year) and included as a variable cost.

To work Problems 7–19:

1. Add the Fixed Cost amounts in the Monthly Cost column to calculate the Total Fixed Costs. Add this amount to the memory.
2. Add the Variable Cost amounts in the Monthly Cost column to calculate the Total Variable Costs. Add this amount to the memory.
3. Recall the memory to obtain the Total Monthly Ownership Cost.
4. Divide each Fixed Cost amount by 1,000 to calculate the Cost per Mile (assuming that 1,000 miles are estimated to be driven each month). Use constant division. Accumulate the amounts in the memory. Refer to Job 8, page 30, for a review of constant division, if necessary.
5. Recall the memory to obtain the Total Fixed Costs, Cost per Mile.
6. Repeat Steps 4 and 5 to calculate the Total Variable Costs, Cost per Mile.
7. Add the Total Fixed Costs, Cost per Mile amount and the Total Variable Costs, Cost per Mile amount to calculate the Total Monthly Ownership Cost, Cost per Mile.

LEARNING OBJECTIVE
Calculate casualty losses.

CASUALTY INSURANCE LOSSES
Casualty insurance is protection against losses from disasters such as fires and floods. Large policies are sometimes divided among several insurance companies so that the losses are shared among them.

To work Problems 1–3:

1. Add the insurance carried by each company (92,706; 137,930; 150,612) to calculate the total amount of insurance carried (381,248.00).
2. Divide the insurance carried by each company by the total insurance carried to calculate the percent of total insurance carried by each company:
   a. Round answers to 6 decimal places.
   b. Use constant division. Refer to Job 8 if necessary.
   c. Accumulate the percent of insurance carried by each company in the memory. Recall the memory to obtain the total percent of insurance carried (1.000001).
3. Multiply the percent of insurance carried by each company by the amount of loss (244,800) to calculate the amount of loss each company will pay:
   a. Round answers to 2 decimal places.
   b. Use constant multiplication. Refer to Job 7 if necessary.
   c. Accumulate the amount of loss to be paid by each company in the memory. Recall the memory to obtain the total amount of losses paid (244,800.24).
4. If the total amount of loss to pay does not equal the amount of loss, calculate the adjusted amount to pay by subtracting the difference (which will be less than $1) from the company that has the largest amount of loss to pay.

NAME_____ DATE_____ PERIOD_____ GRADE_____

Casualty Insurance Losses

	Company A	Company B	Company C	Totals
1. Amount of loss = $244,800				
a. Insurance carried	92,706	137,930	150,612	**a.** 381,248.00
b. % of insurance carried	.243165	.361786	.395050	**b.** 1.000001
c. Amount of loss to pay	59,526.79	88,565.21	96,708.24	**c.** 244,800.24
d. Adjusted amount to pay			96,708.00	
2. Amount of loss = $175,000				
a. Insurance carried	63,000	85,000	75,000	**a.** _____
b. % of insurance carried				**b.** _____
c. Amount of loss to pay				**c.** _____
d. Adjusted amount to pay				
3. Amount of loss = $90,234				
a. Insurance carried	86,650	78,850	82,250	**a.** _____
b. % of insurance carried				**b.** _____
c. Amount of loss to pay				**c.** _____
d. Adjusted amount to pay				

Answers

1a.	$381,248.00
b.	1.000001%
c.	$244,800.24
d.	$96,708.00
2a.	_____
b.	_____
c.	_____
d.	_____
3a.	_____
b.	_____
c.	_____
d.	_____

80% Coinsurance Clause

4. John Thomason insured his house against casualty loss for $75,000. He had a casualty loss of $14,300. How much will John collect if the present value of his house is $155,000? The policy contains an 80% coinsurance clause. _____$8,649.20_____

5. Carol Cowling's house is valued at $120,000. She carries casualty insurance of $85,000 with an 80% coinsurance clause. A fire in Carol's cellar caused damages of $10,700. How much will the insurance company pay? _____

6. A house valued at $92,000 was insured for $76,000. The policy contained an 80% coinsurance clause. A flood caused damages of $78,000.

  a. How much insurance is needed? _____

  b. How much will the company pay? _____

  c. How much will the owner pay? _____

7. Scott Abrams insured his house for $56,000. The insurance policy has an 80% coinsurance clause. It also carries a $250 deductible clause, which means that the company will not pay for $250 of the loss. The house is valued at $85,000. How much of a $5,500 vandalism loss will the company pay? _____

8. Karen Balzen carries $89,900 in tornado insurance on her house and garage. The policy has an 80% coinsurance clause and a $300 deductible clause. The present value of the house is $125,000. How much of a $22,000 tornado loss will the company pay? _____

APPLICATION FOR YOUR LIFE | Insurance Contracts

The terms and provisions of an insurance policy can be lengthy and complicated. If you do not understand the contract, seek help from a competent insurance agent.

Answers

4. _____$8,649.20_____

5. _____

6a. _____

  b. _____

  c. _____

7. _____

8. _____

80% COINSURANCE CLAUSE

Because casualties (losses) seldom result in the complete destruction of a building, few owners carry insurance coverage equal to 100% of a building's value. Most policies contain an **80% coinsurance clause**, which means owners must carry insurance coverage equal to 80% of the value of their building.

To work Problems 4–8:

4. a. Multiply the present value (155,000) by 80% to calculate the insurance needed (124,000.00).
   b. Divide the insurance carried (75,000) by the insurance needed (124,000) to calculate the company's portion (.604839).
   c. Multiply the loss (14,300) by the company's portion (.604839) to calculate the amount collected (8,649.20).

5. Follow the procedure described in Problem 4 to calculate the amount paid by the company.

6. a. Multiply the present value (92,000) by 80% to calculate the insurance needed.
   b. Insurance carried exceeds insurance needed; company pays full amount of coverage.
   c. Loss exceeds coverage; subtract the coverage (76,000) from the loss (78,000) to calculate the amount paid by the owner.

7. a. Multiply the present value (85,000) by 80% to calculate the insurance needed.
   b. Divide the insurance carried (56,000) by the insurance needed (from Step 7a) to calculate the company's portion.
   c. Multiply the loss (5,500) by the company's portion (from Step 7b) to calculate the company's share.
   d. Subtract the deductible (250) from the company's share (from Step 7c) to calculate the amount paid by the company.

8. Follow the procedure described in Problem 7 to calculate the amount paid by the company.

LEARNING OBJECTIVE

Perform calculations involving school-related mathematical problems.

SCHOOL YEAR BUDGET

Jessica's father asked her to prepare a budget for her senior year in high school so that he can estimate his expenses.

To work Problems 1–7:

1. Work the problems in lines a–f.

Line a: An average lunch in high school costs $5.10. Multiply 5.10 × 5 (five school days a week) to calculate the weekly total. Record your answer in Column A. Multiply the weekly total by 36 (36 weeks in a school year) to calculate the yearly total. Record your answer in Column B.

Line b: The gas to drive to school costs $2.75 each day. Multiply 2.75 × 5 to calculate the weekly total, and record your answer in Column A. Multiply the weekly total by 36 to calculate the yearly total, and record your answer in Column B.

Line c: Tickets to sporting events are $4.50 each. Multiply 4.50 × 24 (24 games to attend), and record your answer in Column B.

Line d: Music lessons cost $25.00 each week. Multiply 25.00 × 32, and record your answer in Column B.

Line e: Application fees to colleges are $30.00 each. Multiply 30.00 × 5 (five college applications), and record your answer in Column B.

Line f: Cell phone service costs $50.00 each month. Multiply 50.00 × 9 (nine months in a school year), and record your answer in Column B.

2. Add each amount in Column B (lines a–m) to calculate the total budget for the school year.

School Year Budget

SCHOOL YEAR BUDGET			
Line	**Column A**	**Column B**	
a. Lunch Money $5.10 x 5 =	_____ x 36 =	**1.** _____	
b. Gasoline $2.75 x 5 =	_____ x 36 =	**2.** _____	
c. Tickets $4.50 x 24 =		**3.** _____	
d. Music Lessons $25.00 x 32 =		**4.** _____	
e. Application Fees $30.00 x 5 =		**5.** _____	
f. Cell Phone $50.00 x 9 =		**6.** _____	
g. Car Insurance		1,500.00	
h. Band Trip		150.00	
i. Student Council Camp		110.00	
j. Miscellaneous — Entertainment		864.00	
k. Yearbook		45.00	
l. Class Ring		360.00	
m. Graduation Cap and Gown		42.00	
Total Budget for School Year		**7.** _____	

Answers

1. _____
2. _____
3. _____
4. _____
5. _____
6. _____
7. _____

APPLICATION FOR YOUR LIFE | Estimating

Developing the habit of estimating can start with a school budget. For example, a gasoline cost of $2.75 can be rounded to $3 and multiplied by 5 days a week. You know the answer must be close to $15.

Calculating a Class Grade

Week	Homework Grades	Classwork Grades
2	90	78
4	87	82
6	92	86
8	81	91
10	79	92
12	85	93
14	95	88
16	87	89
18	83	90
	Total **8.** _____	Total **10.** _____
	Average **9.** _____	Average **11.** _____

	Grade Average		Percent of Total Grade	Percent of Grade Average
Homework	_____	x	10%	**12.** _____
Classwork	_____	x	10%	**13.** _____
Test 1	96	x	15%	**14.** _____
Test 2	86	x	15%	**15.** _____
Test 3	90	x	15%	**16.** _____
Test 4	93	x	15%	**17.** _____
			Total **18.** _____	

Final Grade Needed for an A

Line a   90.00

Line b   – _____

Line c   **19.** _____

Line d ÷ 20%   **20.** _____

Final Grade Needed for a B

Line e   80.00

Line f   – _____

Line g   **21.** _____

Line h ÷ 20%   **22.** _____

Answers

8. _____
9. _____
10. _____
11. _____
12. _____
13. _____
14. _____
15. _____
16. _____
17. _____
18. _____
19. _____
20. _____
21. _____
22. _____

CALCULATING A CLASS GRADE

Jessica wants to earn an A in her biology class. Calculate the grade Jessica needs on her final exam to earn an A. The final is worth 20% of her total grade. Also calculate the grade she needs to keep her B. The grading scale at her high school is:

90–100=A   80–89=B   70–79=C   60–69=D   0–59=F

To work Problems 8–18:

1. Add the column of Homework Grades to calculate the Total. Divide the Total by 9 (the number of weekly grades) to calculate the Average. Round the Average to a whole number.
2. Repeat step 1 for the Classwork Grades.
3. Record the Homework and Classwork Averages (answers 9 and 11) in the Grade Average column.
4. Multiply each Grade Average (Homework, Classwork, and Tests 1, 2, 3, and 4) by the corresponding Percent of Total Grade. Round the answers to two decimal places. Add each answer to the memory. Record your answers in the Percent of Grade Average column.
5. Recall the memory to obtain the Total Percent of Grade Average.

To work Problems 19–20:

1. Record the Total Percent of Grade Average (answer 18) on line b. Subtract line b from line a (90.00 is the minimum grade needed for an A). Record your answer on line c.
2. Divide line c by 20% (what the final exam is worth), and record your answer on line d. Jessica needs this grade on her final exam to earn an A in the class.

To work Problems 21–22:

1. Record the Total Percent of Grade Average (answer 18) on line f. Subtract line f from line e (80.00 is the minimum grade needed for a B). Record your answer on line g.
2. Divide line g by 20% and record your answer on line h. Jessica needs this grade on her final exam to earn a B in the class.

NAME_____ DATE_____ PERIOD_____ GRADE_____

CALCULATING A COLLEGE GRADE POINT AVERAGE

Jessica's older brother is calculating his college grade point average (GPA) for the semester. As a second–semester sophomore, his grades are 1/4 of his cumulative GPA. Each letter grade (A, B, C, D, F) is given a number value (4, 3, 2, 1, 0).

SEMESTER GPA

To work Problems 23–30:
1. Multiply the Hours for each class (Column C) by the Number Values (Column B). Record your answers in Column D, Course Points.
2. Add Column C and record the Total.
3. Add Column D and record the Total.
4. Divide the total of Column D by the total of Column C to calculate the fourth semester's GPA. Record your answer in Column D.

OVERALL GPA

To work Problems 31–37:
1. Record the fourth semester's GPA in the GPA for Semester column.
2. Add the first semester's GPA (3.56) to the second semester's GPA (4.00) and record the answer in the Cumulative GPA column (7.56).
3. Add the third semester's GPA to 7.56 and record the new total in the Cumulative GPA column.
4. Add the fourth semester's GPA to the previous answer and record the new total in the Cumulative GPA column.
5. Divide each Cumulative GPA by the Semester Number to calculate the Overall GPA for each semester. Record your answers in the Overall GPA column.

Calculating a College Grade Point Average

Each Semester's Effect on GPA

Semester	Effect on GPA
1	1
2	1/2
3	1/3
4	1/4
5	1/5
6	1/6
7	1/7
8	1/8

Letter Grades and Number Values

Grade		Value
A	=	4
B	=	3
C	=	2
D	=	1
F	=	0

Semester GPA

Semester 4 Courses	(A) Grades	(B) Number Values	(C) Hours	(D) Course Points
Statistics I	A	4	3	23. ____12____
Marketing Research	A	4	3	24. _____
Corporate Finance	B	3	3	25. _____
Business Communication	A	4	3	26. _____
Art History	B	3	3	27. _____
		Totals	28. _____	29. _____
			Semester 4 GPA	30. _____

Overall GPA

Semester Number	GPA for Semester	Cumulative GPA	Overall GPA
1	3.56		34. ___3.56___
2	4.00	31. ___7.56___	35. _____
3	3.40	32. _____	36. _____
4	_____	33. _____	37. _____

Answers

23. ____12____
24. _____
25. _____
26. _____
27. _____
28. _____
29. _____
30. _____
31. ___7.56___
32. _____
33. _____
34. ___3.56___
35. _____
36. _____
37. _____

Earning Money for Expenses

Price of Game System $343.00

Sales Tax (7⅞%) .... **38.** +_____

Total Cost of Game
System .... **39.** _____

	Weekly
Total Earnings.............	$115.00
Car Payment	
($150/month)....... **40.** –	_____
Leisure Money............. –	35.00
Spendable Cash ..... **41.**	_____

Plan A

Total Cost of Game System	÷	Spendable Cash	=	Number of Weeks to Purchase Game System
_____	÷	_____	=	**42.** _____

Plan B

A La Carte Lunch	–	Plate Lunch	=	Amount Saved Daily	x 5 days =	Amount Saved Weekly on Lunches
$5.25	–	$2.70	=	**43.** _____	x 5 days =	**44.** _____

Spendable Cash	+	Amount Saved Weekly on Lunches	=	Total Saved Weekly
_____	+	_____	=	**45.** _____

Total Cost of Game System	÷	Total Saved Weekly	=	Number of Weeks to Purchase Game System
_____	÷	_____	=	**46.** _____

47. Which plan will take Tracy the least amount of time to save enough money to purchase the game system? _____

Answers

38. _____

39. _____

40. _____

41. _____

42. _____

43. _____

44. _____

45. _____

46. _____

47. _____

EARNING MONEY FOR EXPENSES

Tracy earns $115.00 a week, which goes toward her car payment and leisure money. The money left over is spendable cash. Tracy wants to buy a game system with this money.

To work Problems 38–41:

1. Multiply the price of the game system (343.00) by .07875 (7⅞%) to calculate the sales tax.
2. Add the sales tax to $343.00 to calculate the total cost of the game system.
3. Divide the monthly car payment by 4 to calculate the weekly car payment.
4. Subtract the weekly car payment and leisure money from Tracy's weekly total earnings to calculate her weekly spendable cash.

PLAN A

Calculate the number of weeks it will take Tracy to save enough spendable cash to purchase the game system.

To work Problem 42:

Divide the total cost of the game system by the amount of weekly spendable cash.

PLAN B

Calculate the amount Tracy will save each week by eating plate lunches (a set menu usually at a special price) instead of buying her lunch a la carte (each menu item priced separately).

To work Problems 43–47:

1. Subtract the price of a plate lunch (2.70) from the price of an a la carte lunch (5.25) to calculate the amount saved daily.
2. Multiply the amount saved daily by 5 days to calculate the amount saved weekly on lunches.
3. Add the spendable cash to the amount saved weekly on lunches to calculate the total Tracy can save each week with Plan B.
4. Divide the total cost of the game system by the total saved weekly to calculate the number of weeks to purchase the game system.
5. Compare the number of weeks to purchase the game system for each plan. Which plan will take Tracy the least amount of time to purchase the game system?

NAME_____ DATE_____ PERIOD_____ GRADE_____

LEARNING OBJECTIVES

1. Review and improve your ability to solve problems involving a school year budget, casualty insurance losses, housing expenditures, and automobile financing.
2. Increase SAM or decrease EAM to prepare for the Ten-Key Numeric Test (TKNTest).

SKILL BUILDER

To improve your technique, speed, and accuracy, complete the following drills:

1. Technique Drills A–F, page 115.
2. Speed Drills A–E, page 114. Record your scores on the Speed Drill Record.
3. Accuracy Drills A–E, page 112.

REVIEW OF JOBS 26–29

Complete Problems 1–36, which review Jobs 26–29.

Review of Jobs 26–29

School Year Budget

SCHOOL YEAR BUDGET		
Line	Column A	Column B
a. Lunch Money $4.10 x 5 =	_____ x 36 =	**1.** _____
b. Gasoline $2.90 x 5 =	_____ x 36 =	**2.** _____
c. Tickets $5.00 x 26 =		**3.** _____
d. Music Lessons $20.00 x 32 =		**4.** _____
e. Cell Phone $47.00 x 9 =		**5.** _____
f. Car Insurance		1,380.00
g. Band Trip		120.00
h. Student Council Camp		350.00
i. Miscellaneous — Entertainment		1,000.00
Total Budget for School Year		**6.** _____

Casualty Insurance Losses

	Company A	Company B	Company C	Totals
7. Amount of loss = $92,270				
a. Insurance carried	82,458	79,675	85,252	**a.** _____
b. % of insurance carried	_____	_____	_____	**b.** _____
c. Amount of loss to pay	_____	_____	_____	**c.** _____
d. Adjusted amount to pay	_____	_____	_____	

Answers

1. _____
2. _____
3. _____
4. _____
5. _____
6. _____
7a. _____
b. _____
c. _____
d. _____

Housing Expenditures

HOUSING EXPENDITURES Qualifying Incomes			
Qualifying Annual Gross Income	**Maximum House Price**	**Maximum Yearly Expenditure**	**Maximum Monthly Expenditure**
$25,000	8. _____	9. _____	10. _____
35,000	11. _____	12. _____	13. _____
45,000	14. _____	15. _____	16. _____
55,000	17. _____	18. _____	19. _____
65,000	20. _____	21. _____	22. _____
75,000	23. _____	24. _____	25. _____
95,000	26. _____	27. _____	28. _____
100,000	29. _____	30. _____	31. _____

Financing an Automobile

MONTHLY AUTO PAYMENT	
Purchase Cost	**Amount**
a. Sticker Price	$24,500.00
b. Sales Tax	1,531.25
c. Title and Registration	334.76
Total Cost	32. _____
d. Down Payment	1,000.00
Remaining Balance	33. _____
e. APR Financing	1,509.15
Net Cost	34. _____
f. Loan Time	36 months
Monthly Loan Payment	35. _____

36. The buyer wants to know what his monthly payment will be with different loan times. The APR is 3.55%. What is the new monthly payment for a loan of:

a. 48 months with APR financing of $1,997.19? _____

b. 60 months with APR financing of $2,490.39? _____

c. 72 months with APR financing of $2,989.83? _____

Answers

8. _____
9. _____
10. _____
11. _____
12. _____
13. _____
14. _____
15. _____
16. _____
17. _____
18. _____
19. _____
20. _____
21. _____
22. _____
23. _____
24. _____
25. _____
26. _____
27. _____
28. _____
29. _____
30. _____
31. _____
32. _____
33. _____
34. _____
35. _____
36a. _____
  b. _____
  c. _____

TEN-KEY NUMERIC DRILL

Complete TKNDrill #2 on page 117 by following the instructions on page 13.

If you completed Jobs 1–30 in less than 30 hours, repeat them until you complete 30 hours of practice. Do this before you take the TKNTest so that your scores can be compared with others who have completed 30 hours of practice.

Your teacher will administer the TKNTest.

REMEMBER TO:

1. Clear your desk of everything except materials needed for this class.
2. Position this book on your desk at an angle so that you can easily read the numbers and write the answers.
3. Strike each key separately.
4. Use a rhythmic touch.
5. Do not pause between strokes.
6. Keep your eyes on the book. Do not look at the keypad.

Correcting Addition Errors

Problem

| 731 |
| 552 |
| 313 |
| 739 |
| 2,335 |

Incorrect Number
Correction (Subtract)

```
                    0.  CA

          731.  +
          552.  +
     ►    331.  +
     ►    331.  –
          313.  +
          739.  +
        2,335.  *
```

Correcting Addition Errors on the Tape

Problem

| 731 |
| 552 |
| 313 |
| 739 |
| 2,335 |

Incorrect Number

Correction
Correct Answer

```
                    0.  CA

          731.  +
          552.  +
     ►    303.  +
                      x10
          739.  +

        2,325.  *
     ►              +10
     ►            2,335
```

Correcting Subtraction Errors on the Tape

Problem

| 767 |
| –347 |
| 694 |
| –423 |
| 691 |

Incorrect Number

Correction
Correct Answer

```
                    0.  CA

          767.  +
     ►    357.  –
                      x10
          694.  +
          423.  –
          681.  *
     ►              +10
     ►              691
```

Correcting Subtraction Errors

Problem

| 767 |
| –347 |
| 694 |
| –423 |
| 691 |

Incorrect Number
Correction (Add)

```
                    0.  CA

          767.  +
     ►    357.  –
     ►    357.  +
          347.  –
          694.  +
          423.  –
          691.  *
```

Problem

| 914 |
| 316 |
| 858 |
| 375 |
| 2,463 |

Incorrect Number

Correction
Correct Answer

```
                    0.  CA

          914.  +
     ►    361.  +
                      +45
          858.  +
          375.  +

        2,508.  *
     ►              –45
     ►            2,463
```

Problem

| 389 |
| –151 |
| 644 |
| –281 |
| 601 |

Incorrect Number

Correction
Correct Answer

```
                    0.  CA

          389.  +
          151.  –
          644.  +
     ►    271.  –
                      –10
          611.  *
     ►              –10
     ►              601
```

CORRECTING CALCULATING ERRORS

If you make an error while working a problem, it will be necessary to make corrections. Correct errors following the instructions in the subheadings below that apply to your calculator and the type of error.

Calculator With Tape (Printing)

1. ***Before* a Number is Printed on the Tape**

   If an error is detected before a function key (any key other than a number key, including the +, –, ×, and .) is struck:

   a. Strike the Clear Key [4] to clear the incorrect number from the display window. Your calculator may have a Clear Right Digit Key [5] in addition to a Clear Key. Strike the Clear Right Digit Key to clear an incorrect digit at the right of a number. For example, if you enter 456 rather than 453, the Clear Right Digit Key will clear the 6 from the display window rather than the entire number.

   b. Enter the correct number.

2. ***After* a Number Has Been Printed on the Tape**

   a. *Before* a Total Has Been Taken

   If an error is detected after a function key has been struck but before a total has been taken:

   (1) Subtract (if the incorrect number was added) or add (if the incorrect number was subtracted) the incorrect number to cancel the error.

   (2) Enter the correct number.

   b. *After* a Total Has Been Taken

If an error is detected after a function key has been struck and after a total has been taken:

(1) Tear your tape from the calculator and place it beside the problem. Compare the numbers on the tape with the numbers in the problem. Find the omitted, extra, or incorrect number(s).

(2) Write the amount of the error and how to correct it to the right of the incorrect number on the tape. Add or subtract the amount of the error from the total.

Calculator Without Tape (Display)

1. **_Before_ a Number is Entered Into the Register**

   If an error is detected before a function key is struck:

   a. Strike the Clear Key [4] to clear the incorrect number from the display window. Your calculator may have a Clear Right Digit Key [5] in addition to a Clear Key. Strike the Clear Right Digit Key to clear an incorrect digit at the right of a number. For example, if you enter 456 rather than 453, the Clear Right Digit Key will clear the 6 from the display window rather than the entire number.

   b. Enter the correct number.

2. **_After_ a Number Has Been Entered Into the Register**

   If an error is detected after a function key has been struck:

   a. Subtract (if the incorrect number was added) or add (if the incorrect number was subtracted) the incorrect number to cancel the error.

   b. Enter the correct number.

Correcting Omitted and Extra Numbers on the Tape

Problem

276
331
480
825
——
1,912

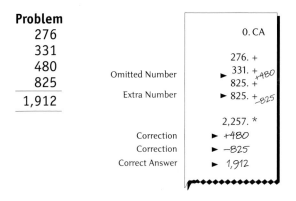

Omitted Number

Extra Number

Correction
Correction
Correct Answer

CORRECTING ADDITION ERRORS		CORRECTING SUBTRACTION ERRORS	
Problem	**Display**	**Problem**	**Display**
543	543	462	462
489	Incorrect Number ▶ 498	692	692
651	Correction (Subtract) ▶ −498	−179	Incorrect Number ▶ −197
201	489	−288	Correction (Add) ▶ +197
1,884	651	687	−179
	201		−288
	1,884		687

1. *General Rules*
   a. The number of strokes to count for a problem cannot exceed the number of strokes (50) in the original problem.
   b. Count one error per addend.

Type of Error	Strokes to Count	Errors to Count
2. *Incorrect Entries*		
a. Strikes wrong function key (Example: x, +, Non-Add, Grand Total).	0	0 if it does not affect answer; 1 error per problem if it affects answer
b. Enters incorrect addend twice.	0	1 for first incorrect addend; 1 for repetition
c. Enters incorrect addend, doesn't subtract it, then enters correct addend.	Only strokes for correct addend	1 for incorrect addend
d. Enters incorrect addend.	Deduct strokes for omitted digits; count strokes for added digits	1
3. *Omissions*		
a. Omits entire problem.	0	1 for omission
b. Omits an addend.	Deduct all strokes in omitted addend	1 for each addend omitted
c. Partially completed problem:		
(1) When time is called.	All strokes entered	All committed; no error for not completing problem
(2) When the problem is not the final problem for the attempt and the student either strikes the Total Key, stops and starts over, or continues to the next problem.	All	All committed; 1 for stopping
d. Omits the remaining addends in the final problem on the tape, then strikes the Total Key.	All	0
4. *Additions and/or Repeats*		
a. Enters total as an addend.	0	1
b. Enters correct addend twice.	0	1 for repetition
c. Repeats entire problem.	All strokes for both problems	1 for repetition; all errors in both problems
5. *Corrected Errors*		
Corrects error and gets correct answer.	No strokes for correcting error	0
6. *Calculator Operations That Do Not Affect SAM or EAM Productivity*		
a. Numbers the problems.	0	0
b. Clears the calculator between attempts.	0	0
c. Does not clear the calculator between attempts.	0	0
d. Strikes Add Key and answer prints twice.	0	0
e. Strikes Non-Add Key within problem.	0	0
f. Enters incorrect addend, then subtracts it.	0	0

DECIMAL ROUNDING RULES

Study the decimal rounding rules carefully and refer to them when necessary as you complete the problems in each calculating job. Where applicable, set the Decimal Place Selector before you work each problem; each answer will then be automatically rounded to the desired decimal place.

1. Round all answers to two decimal places unless otherwise instructed. If your calculator does not automatically round to the desired decimal place, it may be necessary to manually round the number. For example, to round a product to two decimal places, at least three decimal places are needed in the answer. If the number in the third decimal place is 5 or more, the number in the second decimal place is increased by 1.

   Example: $\begin{array}{r} 1.23 \\ \times\ .3 \\ \hline .369 \end{array}$ = .37

   If the number in the third decimal place is 4 or less, the number in the second decimal place is not changed.

   Example: $\begin{array}{r} 7.21 \\ \times\ .3 \\ \hline 2.163 \end{array}$ = 2.16

   a. Decimals can be rounded to any place using this procedure.
   b. The 5/4 position on the Decimal Rounding Selector automatically rounds answers to the decimal place specified on the Decimal Place Selector setting.

2. In answers involving dollars and cents, always round the answer to two decimal places.

   Example: $1.296 = $1.30

3. In answers expressed as percents, round the answer to four decimal places unless otherwise instructed. Convert the answer to a percent by moving the decimal two places to the right.

   Example: .29667 = .2967 = 29.67%

4. In problems converting fractions to decimal equivalents, round the decimal equivalent to four decimal places.

   Example: 2/3 = .666667 = .6667

5. In problems involving decimals that will be multiplied by a whole number (such as chain discounts and multiple operations), round the decimal factor to four places.

   Example: 29.6666666 = 29.6667

6. In problems with a series of answers in dollars and cents (such as invoices with extensions, totals, discounts, and taxes), round each arithmetical operation to dollars and cents.

   Example:
2 1/2 doz. @ $.37	= $ .925	= $ .93
6 doz. @ $.209	= $1.254	= $1.25
Subtotal		= $2.18
Plus 5% tax = $.109	= $ .11	= $ .11
Total		= $2.29

FEATURES

The display and display-print features of the calculator are listed below. The Applications section on this page summarizes when to apply each feature.

Display Features

1. A running total (accumulation of all previous calculations) is displayed without striking the Total Key.
2. Each entry is shown so that the operator can check and correct the entry before it is transferred into the operating register of the calculator.
3. Paper is saved.
4. Numbers in the display window are usually easier to see than the numbers on the tape because they are larger and in a more prominent location on the calculator.
5. Use of the display is quieter than the tape.

Display-Print Features

1. A mistake can be traced by comparing the numbers on the tape with the numbers in the book.
2. The tape can be saved as a reference.
3. Time is saved in recording answers. The operator can work all problems before taking his or her fingers off the home row to record answers. Thus, the chance of misplacing fingers on the keys is reduced.
4. The tape allows the operator to see the last number entered into the register so work can be resumed easily after an interruption.

APPLICATIONS

Follow these guidelines to determine when to use the display only and when to use the display-print feature:

1. Display only
   a. Few entries are required. (Examples: subtraction, multiplication, or division problems.)
   b. A record on tape is not needed.
2. Display-Print
   a. Many entries are required. (Examples: addition; mixed operations such as an invoice using multiplication, addition, and subtraction.)
   b. A record on tape is needed.

PROVING ANSWERS

To prove an answer means to check an answer that you have calculated. *You should prove all your answers if the book does not provide the correct answer.*

1. Work the problem and record your first answer on the blank line near the problem.
2. Work the problem a second time. If your second answer is:
   a. the same as the first, assume it is correct. Record the answer in the answer column and work the next problem.
   b. different from the first:

Display: Work the problem until you calculate two answers that match. You may assume these matching answers are correct.

Display-Print: Proofread by comparing numbers on your tape with the problem in the book. If the numbers on the tape match the numbers in the book, assume the answer on the tape is correct. If the numbers on the tape do not match the numbers in the book, correct the error(s) on the tape (see page 106, *Correcting Calculating Errors*).

VERIFYING ANSWERS

To verify an answer means to compare your answer with the answer provided by *someone else*; in this case, the answer in the book.

1. Work the problem. If your answer is:
   a. the same as the book's, assume it is correct and record it in the answer column.
   b. different from the book's:

Display: Work the problem until you calculate two answers that match. You may assume these matching answers are correct.

Display-Print: Compare the numbers on your tape with the problem in the book, and correct the error on the tape or in the book.

PROVING ANSWERS (CHECKING YOUR OWN ANSWER)			
If the Problem Was Completed Using	**On the Second Attempt Use**	**If Answer Matches**	**If Answer Does Not Match**
Display only (few entries)	Display only	Record answer	Rework on display until answers match
Display-Print (many entries)	Display only	Record answer	Compare tape from first attempt against book

VERIFYING ANSWERS (CHECKING SOMEONE ELSE'S ANSWER)		
If the Problem Was Completed Using	**If Answer Matches**	**If Answer Does Not Match**
Display only	Record answer	Rework on display until answers match
Display-Print	Record answer	Compare tape from first attempt against book

LEARNING OBJECTIVE

As you work each Accuracy Drill, concentrate only on accuracy; ignore speed. If you have time, repeat the drills.

DRILL A

Your speed should be reduced because no key is adjacent to the next key in each addend. Work the problem until you complete it without an error.

DRILL B

This problem contains digits within addends that have similar configurations. For example, rounded digits (3, 6, 0, 9) and straight digits (1, 4, 7). Your speed should be reduced because you must distinguish between similar digits. Work the problem until you complete it without an error.

DRILL C

This problem contains handwritten digits. Because handwriting can be somewhat difficult to read, you will need to reduce your speed. Work the problem until you complete it without an error.

DRILL D

Concentrate on maintaining accuracy with stamina. Keep your eyes on the digits in the problem. Work the problem until you complete it without an error.

DRILL E

Each of these five problems has the same answer: 77,777.

1. Work Problem 1.
   a. If your answer is correct, continue to Step 2.
   b. If your answer is not correct, repeat the problem until you calculate the correct answer.
2. Work Problems 1 through 5 following the procedure in Step 1 until all problems are correct in the *same* attempt. For example, if you make an error in Problem 4, start again with Problem 1.

(A)	(B)	(C)	(D)
76,261	3,608	29,531	2,428
3,427	33,960	838,763	59,614
138,160	4,141	4,120	623,737
50,834	71,441	265,468	265
372,617	225	91,722	152,842
40,371	2,552	353,061	21,936
2,768	339	4,895	17,215
505,194	69,889	28,361	3,149
1,189,632	186,155	1,615,921	687,997
			6,672
			52,193
			122,852
			644
			17,463
			53,419
			684,736
			9,867
			39,138
			6,457
			23,172
			56,726
			108,951
			10,634
			165,914
			243,665
			3,171,686

(E)

1.	2.	3.	4.	5.
6,641	17,231	31,998	25,961	6,732
34,129	834	3,087	4,722	2,985
2,780	1,937	12,356	11,490	14,037
582	6,848	9,973	9,584	562
11,946	523	463	147	10,983
1,308	45,712	10,857	855	8,221
13,552	3,687	1,684	17,278	4,215
6,839	1,005	7,359	7,740	30,042
77,777	77,777	77,777	77,777	77,777

Test No.	Date	(1) Number of Errors	(2) Deduction for Each Error	(3) Total Error Deduction (1) x (2)	(4) Accuracy Grade 100 – (3)	(5) Accuracy Grade Doubled (4) x 2	(6) Time	(7) Time Grade	(8) Total Accuracy and Time Grade (5) + (7)	(9) Average of Accuracy and Time Grade (8) ÷ 3
Sample	9/30/--	2	7	14	86	172	30	70	242	81
1										
2										
3										
4										
5										
6										
Final										

(1) Record the Number of Errors you made on the Progress Test.

(2) Record the number of points that your instructor tells you to deduct for each error.

(3) Multiply the Number of Errors by the Deduction for Each Error (1) x (2) to calculate the Total Error Deduction.

(4) Subtract the Total Error Deduction from 100 to calculate the Accuracy Grade.

(5) Multiply the Accuracy Grade by 2 to calculate the Accuracy Grade Doubled. The Accuracy Grade is worth twice as much as Time; therefore, you should strive for accuracy. No matter how fast you solve the problem, the answer is of no value in business if it is not correct.

(6) Record the Time it took you to finish the test.

(7) Your instructor will provide your Time Grade.

(8) Add the Accuracy Grade Doubled to the Time Grade (5) + (7) to calculate the Total Accuracy and Time Grade.

(9) a. Divide the Total Accuracy and Time Grade by 3 (two grades for accuracy and one for time) to calculate the Average of Accuracy and Time Grade. Record the grade in numerals, such as "81," instead of letters, such as "B."

b. When you have calculated the Average of Accuracy and Time Grade for each Progress Test, add the grades in (9) to calculate the Total Grade. Record the Total Grade in the space provided.

c. Divide the Total Grade by the number of test grades that you have to calculate the Average Grade. Record the Average Grade in the space provided.

d. In the Grading Scale, find the letter that corresponds with your Average Grade. Record your Final Grade in the space provided.

Grading Scale		
A = 90 – 100 B = 80 – 89 C = 70 – 79 D = 60 – 69 F = 59 and below	**Total Grade**	
	÷ by_____ equals Average Grade	
	Final Grade	

LEARNING OBJECTIVE

As you work each Speed Drill, concentrate only on speed; ignore errors. If you have time, repeat the drills.

DRILL A

Work the problem as many times as possible in one minute. Determine your SAM by counting one stroke for each digit, Add Key, and Total Key on the tape. Record your SAM on the Speed Drill Record beside the appropriate job number.

DRILL B

Work the problem as many times as possible in one minute. Determine your SAM. Record your SAM on the Speed Drill Record.

DRILL C

This problem has connectors, which means that the last digit in an addend (1,45<u>6</u>) is the first digit in the next addend (<u>6</u>83,774). Work the problem as many times as possible in one minute. Record your SAM.

DRILL D

This problem does not have connectors. Work the problem as many times as possible in one minute. Record your SAM.

DRILL E

Concentrate on maintaining speed with stamina. Work the problem as many times as possible in *three minutes*. Divide total strokes by three minutes to calculate your SAM. Record your SAM.

(A)
111
222
333
444
20 Strokes ⟶ 555
666
777
888
999
000
40 Strokes ⟶ 4,995

(B)
123
456
789
100
20 Strokes ⟶ 123
456
789
100
123
45
40 Strokes ⟶ 3,104

(C)
1,456
683,774
45,046
25 Strokes ⟶ 621,547
7,253
331,014
49,489
90,265
50 Strokes ⟶ 1,829,844

(D)
5,429
368,472
46,504
25 Strokes ⟶ 265,170
9,531
730,143
84,260
10,652
50 Strokes ⟶ 1,520,161

(E)
1,538
59,614
623,737
5,265
30 Strokes ⟶ 152,842
21,936
17,215
23,149
687,997
30 Strokes ⟶ 6,672
52,193
122,852
4,389
17,463
30 Strokes ⟶ 53,419
684,736
59,867
39,138
6,457
30 Strokes ⟶ 23,172
6,726
108,951
1,063
165,914
4,366
150 Strokes ⟶ 2,950,671

Speed Drill Record

Job	Date	A	B	C	D	E
Sample	9/6	110	115	108	106	98
4						
5						
6						
7						
8						
9						
10						
11						
12						
13						
15						
16						
17						
18						
20						
25						
30						

LEARNING OBJECTIVE

As you work each Technique Drill, concentrate so you can develop smooth, rhythmic touch techniques. Work each drill once; do not correct errors. If you have time, repeat the drills.

DRILL A

Tap the Add Key without breaking your rhythm for entering numbers.

DRILL B

Visualize the keypad and concentrate on the location of each key as you strike it. Keep your eyes on your book.

DRILL C

Tap each key with a bouncy, rhythmic stroke.

DRILL D

Concentrate on moving your fingers vertically from one key to the next. Curl your fingers to minimize arm movement.

DRILL E

Try to maintain your rhythm throughout the problem as you move from one addend to the next. Your goal is to maintain your stamina (and breath) until the last addend is entered. Problems with fewer addends should now seem easier to complete.

DRILL F

Keep your eyes on the digits in the problem. Try to maintain your stamina until the last addend is entered. Problems with fewer addends should now seem easier to complete.

(A)	(B)	(C)	(D)	(E)	(F)
1	111	123	369	123	1,538
2	222	456	852	456	59,614
3	333	789	104	789	623,737
4	444	100	785	456	265
5	555	123	236	123	152,842
6	666	456	985	789	21,936
7	777	789	200	456	17,215
8	888	100	104	789	3,149
9	999	2,936	3,635	123	687,997
0	100			456	6,672
45	5,095			123	52,193
				789	122,852
				123	389
				456	17,463
				789	53,419
				456	684,736
				789	9,867
				456	39,138
				123	6,457
				789	23,172
				456	56,726
				789	108,951
				123	10,634
				456	165,914
				789	243,665
				12,066	3,170,541

Illus. A-1
Keep your fingers curved over the home-row keys.

Technique Checklist, Ten-Key Numeric Touch Method

Operator _____ Evaluator _____

Place a check mark (✓) after a technique that is performed satisfactorily. Place a zero (0) after a technique that needs improvement.

Technique	Job	3	4	5	6	7	8	9	10	11	12	13	15	16	17	18	20
	Date																
Getting Ready																	
1. Clears the desk of everything except materials needed for operating the calculator.																	
2. Places the calculator in a position that allows the wrist and hand to be parallel to the keypad and allows the greatest freedom of finger movement over the keypad.																	
3. Positions the book and the calculator at a comfortable angle so numbers can be read and written easily.																	
4. Determines proper settings for decimals.																	
5. Sits in a comfortable position with back straight and feet flat on the floor for proper balance and minimum fatigue.																	
6. Holds the operating wrist straight.																	
7. Curves the fingers of the operating hand.																	
8. Clears the register before starting a problem.																	
9. Has pencil at hand, ready to record answers.																	
Entering Numbers																	
1. Uses a rhythmic, bouncy touch.																	
2. Does not pause between strokes.																	
3. Strikes keys with a firm, quick stroke.																	
4. Keeps eyes on the book and uses the touch method. Does not look at the keypad of the calculator.																	
Proving Answers																	
1. Writes the answers legibly in the proper place.																	
2. Records decimals in answers accurately.																	
3. Corrects calculating errors in the prescribed manner.																	
4. Proves the answers in the prescribed manner.																	
Attitude																	
1. Enthusiastic about learning.																	
2. Optimistic about improving.																	
3. Confident about success.																	
4. Alert but relaxed.																	

(A)	(B)	(C)	(D)	(E)
8,297	645,916	475,932	38,628	402,389
312,509	6,302	98,451	5,748	35,715
82,573	87,409	211,975	342,161	2,830
360,906	185,284	2,368	469,197	876,841
889,356	75,422	82,571	7,419	57,406
753,542	869,514	4,087	51,837	81,657
641	53,277	90,113	16,323	7,430
82,824	4,975	782,341	758,927	589,918
2,490,648	1,928,099	1,747,838	1,690,240	2,054,186

25 strokes (after row 4), *50 strokes* (at total)

(F)	(G)	(H)	(I)	(J)
325,389	664,513	52,883	5,798	33,241
509,738	96,364	156,751	971,486	931,229
7,654	84,722	720,598	31,264	57,692
14,816	59,503	3,107	447,428	60,946
730,259	284,472	8,539	95,387	57,252
186,872	7,845	145,249	15,245	492,963
43,497	96,214	78,984	193,531	82,742
562	48,242	15,643	6,461	2,976
1,818,787	1,341,875	1,181,754	1,766,600	1,719,041

25 strokes (after row 4), *50 strokes* (at total)

(K)	(L)	(M)	(N)	(O)
71,081	529,174	26,378	718,295	168,592
134,509	2,036	268,829	2,165	77,193
3,422	65,124	4,875	367,921	5,712
349,605	181,787	749,321	84,946	205,068
9,166	54,519	135,182	751,322	4,620
74,189	407,841	6,285	16,862	590,492
205,923	8,535	44,617	1,044	339,976
73,596	78,145	70,325	46,909	7,596
921,491	1,327,161	1,305,812	1,989,464	1,399,249

25 strokes (after row 4), *50 strokes* (at total)

TKNDrill Record

(1) Divide Total Strokes by 3 to get Actual SAM.

(2) Divide Total Errors by 3 to get Actual EAM.

(3) Record the best of the three attempts here and on the Drill Graphs on page 119.

(4) Set your Goals, starting with Job 4, *before* beginning the TKNDrill by following these instructions. On the previous TKNDrill, if you made:

a. .33 EAM or fewer, increase your SAM goal 10 strokes higher than the score for your best attempt on the previous TKNDrill and set EAM at .33. (For example, the goals for the sample line are at 99 SAM and .33 EAM.)

b. more than .33 EAM, set your EAM goal at .33 and set SAM the same as on the previous TKNDrill.

Job	Date	Attempt	Total Strokes	(1) Actual SAM	Total Errors	(2) Actual EAM	(3) Best of 3 Attempts SAM	EAM	(4) Goals SAM	EAM	Comments
Sample	9/6	1 2 3	230 275 267	77 92 89	2 3 1	.67 1.00 .33	89	.33	99	.33	*Keep eyes on copy to decrease EAM*
3		1 2 3							No goals for Job 3		
4		1 2 3									
5		1 2 3									
6		1 2 3									
7		1 2 3									
8		1 2 3									
9		1 2 3									
10		1 2 3									
11		1 2 3									
12		1 2 3									
13		1 2 3									
15		1 2 3									
16		1 2 3									
17		1 2 3									
18		1 2 3									
20		1 2 3									

DRILL GRAPH—SAM

The purpose of this graph is to chart your Strokes a Minute progress. Get your SAM from the Best of 3 Attempts column on the TKNDrill Record, page 118.

For Job 3, place a dot where the vertical and horizontal lines intersect for the Job Number and SAM. (The sample line shows a dot for Job 3 at 106 SAM.)

For the remaining jobs, follow the procedure for Job 3 above. (The sample line shows a dot for Job 4 at 123 SAM.) Connect the dots with a line from the previous job to the present job. Progress in increasing Strokes a Minute will be shown by an upward sloping line.

TKNDrill Graph—SAM

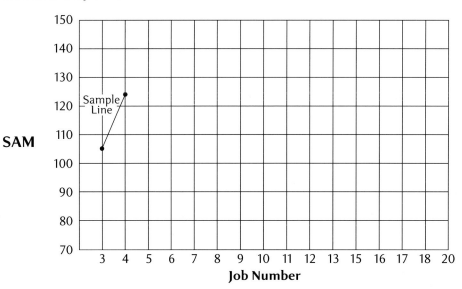

DRILL GRAPH—EAM

The purpose of this graph is to chart your Errors a Minute progress. Get your EAM from the Best of 3 Attempts column on the TKNDrill Record, page 118.

For Job 3, place a dot where the vertical and horizontal lines intersect for the Job Number and EAM. (The sample line shows a dot for Job 3 at 2.00 EAM.)

For the remaining jobs, follow the procedure for Job 3 above. (The sample line shows a dot for Job 4 at 1.67 EAM.) Connect the dots with a line from the previous job to the present job. Progress in reducing Errors a Minute will be shown by a downward sloping line.

TKNDrill Graph—EAM

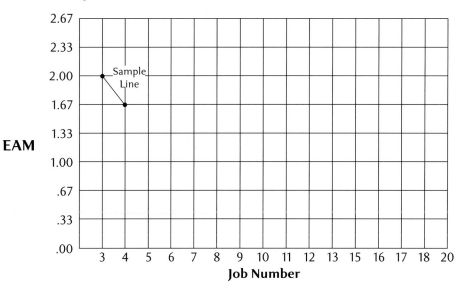

TKNTest Record

Test After	Date	Attempt	Total Strokes	Actual SAM	Total Errors	Actual EAM	Best of 3 Attempts		(1) Goals		Grades			
							SAM	EAM	SAM	EAM	(2) SAM	(2) EAM	(3) Total	(4) Final
Sample	10/19	1 2 3	200 216 249	67 72 83	4 2 1	1.33 .67 .33	83	.33	93	.33	75	90	165	83
Job 5		1 2 3												
Job 10		1 2 3												
Job 15		1 2 3												
Job 20		1 2 3												
Job 25		1 2 3												
Job 30		1 2 3												

(1) To set your goals, follow the instructions for the TKNDrill Record on page 118.

(2) Your instructor will provide information for these grades.

(3) Add grades for SAM and EAM to get the Total grade.

(4) Divide Total by 2 to get the Final grade.

CHAIN DISCOUNT NET EQUIVALENTS

To complete a problem using the Chain Discount Net Equivalents Table:

Example: $43.25 less 15% – 10% – 5%

1. Locate the column headed by 15 (the first discount in the chain) opposite Rate % in the table.
2. Look down that column to where 15 intersects with 10 5 in the left column. The net decimal equivalent of 15% – 10% – 5% is .72675.
3. Multiply the net decimal equivalent (.72675) by the amount ($43.25) to calculate the net amount ($31.43).

Rate %	5	10	12½	15	20	22½	25	30	45
Net	.95	.90	.875	.85	.80	.775	.75	.70	.55
2½	.92625	.8775	.85313	.82875	.78	.75563	.73125	.6825	.53625
5	.9025	.855	.83125	.8075	.76	.73625	.7125	.665	.5225
5 2½	.87994	.83363	.84047	.78731	.741	.71784	.69469	.64838	.50944
5 5	.85738	.81225	.78969	.76713	.722	.69944	.67688	.63175	.49638
5 5 2½	.83594	.79194	.76995	.74795	.70395	.68195	.65995	.61596	.48397
7½	.87875	.8325	.80938	.78625	.74	.71688	.69375	.6475	.50876
7½ 2½	.85678	.81169	.78914	.76659	.72125	.69895	.67641	.63131	.49603
7½ 5	.83481	.79088	.76891	.74694	.703	.68103	.65906	.61513	.48331
10	.855	.81	.7875	.765	.72	.6975	.675	.63	.495
10 2½	.83363	.78975	.76781	.74588	.702	.68006	.65813	.61425	.48263
10 5	.81225	.7695	.74813	.72675	.684	.66263	.64125	.5985	.47025

DECIMAL EQUIVALENTS OF FRACTIONS

The decimal equivalent of a fraction can be determined using the Decimal Equivalents of Fractions Table.

The numbers across the top of the Decimal Equivalents table are numerators (upper number in a fraction).

Numerator ⟶ $\dfrac{5}{}$

The numbers in the left column are denominators (lower number in a fraction).

Denominator ⟶ $\dfrac{}{8}$

To determine the decimal equivalent of 5/8, locate the 5 column under the Numerators heading of the Decimal Equivalents table. Look down the Numerators column to where 5 intersects with 8 in the Denominators column. The equivalent of 5/8 is .625.

| | | NUMERATORS | | | | | | | |
DENOMINATORS		$\dfrac{1}{}$	$\dfrac{2}{}$	$\dfrac{3}{}$	$\dfrac{4}{}$	$\dfrac{5}{}$	$\dfrac{6}{}$	$\dfrac{7}{}$	$\dfrac{8}{}$
	$\dfrac{}{3}$	.33333	.66667						
	$\dfrac{}{4}$	.25	.5	.75					
	$\dfrac{}{5}$	.2	.4	.6	.8				
	$\dfrac{}{6}$	.16667	.33333	.5	.66667	.83333			
	$\dfrac{}{7}$	.14286	.28571	.42857	.57143	.71429	.85714		
	$\dfrac{}{8}$	.125	.25	.375	.5	.625	.75	.875	
	$\dfrac{}{9}$	.11111	.22222	.33333	.44444	.55556	.66667	.77778	.88889
	$\dfrac{}{10}$	.1	.2	.3	.4	.5	.6	.7	.8
	$\dfrac{}{11}$	.09091	.18182	.27273	.36364	.45455	.54546	.63636	.72727
	$\dfrac{}{12}$	.08333	.16667	.25	.33333	.41667	.5	.58333	.66667

INSTRUCTIONAL PATTERN FOR WARM-UP DRILLS

The Instructional Pattern for Warm-Up Drills is outlined in the illustration at right. Practice Warm-Up Drills before each job to develop the ability to move easily from one key to another.

INSTRUCTIONAL PATTERN FOR DRILLS

The Instructional Pattern for Measurement, Technique, Speed, and Accuracy Drills is outlined on page 124. When you work the drills as assigned in the book, you will improve your ten-key touch method proficiency.

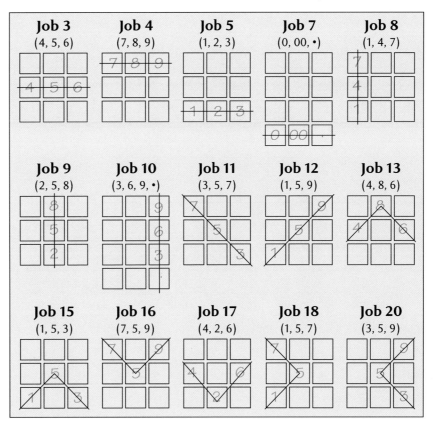

Illus. A-2
Instructional Pattern for Warm-Up Drills.

Instructional Pattern for Measurement, Technique, Speed, and Accuracy Drills

DRILL	1	2	3	4	5	6	7	8	9	10	11	12	13	14	15	16	17	18	19	20	21	22	23	24	25	26	27	28	29	30
MEASUREMENT																														
Pretest, Manual Math	First week and last week of the course																													
Ten-Key Numeric Drill			3	4	5	6	7	8	9	10	11	12	13		15	16	17	18		20					25					30
Ten-Key Numeric Test					5					10					15					20					25					30
Progress Test					5					10					15					20					25					30
TECHNIQUE																														
Warm-Up Drill			3	4	5	6	7	8	9	10	11	12	13		15	16	17	18		20										
1, 2, 3... (Drill A)				4	5	6	7	8	9	10	11	12	13		15	16	17	18		20					25					30
111, 222... (Drill B)				4	5	6	7	8	9	10	11	12	13		15	16	17	18		20					25					30
123, 456... (Drill C)				4	5	6	7	8	9	10	11	12	13		15	16	17	18		20					25					30
Vertical movement of fingers (Drill D)				4	5	6	7	8	9	10	11	12	13		15	16	17	18		20					25					30
Stamina, rhythm 123, 456... (Drill E)				4	5	6	7	8	9	10	11	12	13		15	16	17	18		20					25					30
Stamina, concentration (Drill F)				4	5	6	7	8	9	10	11	12	13		15	16	17	18		20					25					30
SPEED																														
111, 222... (Drill A)				4	5	6	7	8	9	10	11	12	13		15	16	17	18		20					25					30
123, 456... (Drill B)				4	5	6	7	8	9	10	11	12	13		15	16	17	18		20					25					30
Adjacent keys; connectors (Drill C)				4	5	6	7	8	9	10	11	12	13		15	16	17	18		20					25					30
Adjacent keys; no connectors (Drill D)				4	5	6	7	8	9	10	11	12	13		15	16	17	18		20					25					30
Stamina, concentration (Drill E)				4	5	6	7	8	9	10	11	12	13		15	16	17	18		20					25					30
ACCURACY																														
Non-adjacent key reaches; no connectors (Drill A)				4	5	6	7	8	9	10	11	12	13		15	16	17	18		20					25					30
Similar configuration of digits (Drill B)				4	5	6	7	8	9	10	11	12	13		15	16	17	18		20					25					30
Handwritten digits (Drill C)				4	5	6	7	8	9	10	11	12	13		15	16	17	18		20					25					30
Stamina, concentration (Drill D)				4	5	6	7	8	9	10	11	12	13		15	16	17	18		20					25					30
Five problems with same answer: 77,777 (Drill E)				4	5	6	7	8	9	10	11	12	13		15	16	17	18		20					25					30

Instructional Patterns to Individualize Learning

The modular, flexible nature of the text-workbook makes it possible to individualize learning based on:
1. Objective of instruction.
2. The abilities and needs of students enrolled in the course.
3. The amount of time available for instruction.

Objective of Instruction	Jobs to Complete	Problems to Complete	Tests			Drills			
			Pre	Progress	Ten-Key Numeric	Warm-Up	Technique, Speed, Accuracy	Ten-Key Numeric	Production
1. Comprehensive and extensive instruction	All	All	Yes	All	All	All	All	All	All
2. Develop touch method only[1]	1–6	All	Yes	No. 1	All	Jobs 3–6	All	All	None
3. Develop touch method, multiplication, division, and memory[2]	1–10	All	Yes	Nos. 1 & 2	All	Jobs 3–10	All	All	Job 14
4. Comprehensive instruction, limited time	All	Only odd or only even numbered problems	Yes	All	All	All	All	All	All
5. Comprehensive instruction, very limited time	All	First two problems in each section of each Job[3]	Yes	All	All	None	None	None	None
6. Intensive speed and accuracy development	1–20	All	Yes	Nos. 1–4	All	All	All	All	All
7. Improve arithmetic	1–20	All	Yes[4]	None	None	None	None	None	None

[1]This pattern is appropriate for developing touch method mastery for use on the computer numeric pad and other ten-key keypads.

[2]This pattern is appropriate for developing touch method mastery and basic math functions needed for operating calculators in business courses such as Accounting, Business Math, Consumer Math, Record Keeping, and General Business.

[3]For example: In Job 6, Problems 1 and 2, 7 and 8, 10 and 11, 15 and 16, 21 and 22, etc.

[4]Give arithmetic review and administer the Arithmetic Pretest several times to measure the student's competency in arithmetic.

WRITING NUMBERS LEGIBLY AND NUMERIC KEYPAD
Ten-Key Numeric Touch Method

WRITING NUMBERS LEGIBLY

In business, your numbers must be clear and legible so that you and others can read them quickly and correctly. To avoid mistakes, take the time to form your numbers carefully.

When numbers are not written legibly, it is difficult to determine what numbers the writing represents. For example, in Column II write the numbers you believe are represented in Column I. Your instructor can tell you what numbers the writing in Column I represents.

Column I	Column II
981	_____
015	_____
777	_____
190	_____
481	_____
110	_____
645	_____
Total 4,768	_____

Sometimes it is possible to determine an illegible number by checking other sources. For example, in Column I the total is distinguishable. You could determine the numbers for each addend, after trying enough combinations of guessing, and get them to total 4,768. But this process takes unnecessary time. Write numbers legibly so that you and others can read them rapidly and accurately.

To help you learn to write numbers legibly, complete the following exercise:

1. Write the numbers 0 through 9 on the line below.

_____

2. Now compare your numbers with the Number Legibility Scale below.
   a. Are all numbers the same size?
   b. Are the lines straight in 1, 4, 7, and 9?
   c. Are the angles in 4, 5, and 7 corners and not rounded?
   d. Are the circles in 6, 8, 9, and 0 closed at the intersection?
   e. Are the sizes of the numbers and the spaces between numbers adjusted to fit the length of the line on which they are written?
3. Writing legible numbers requires constant attention and careful practice. Practice again writing legibly the numbers 0 through 9 until they are written as well as examples A or B in the Number Legibility Scale.

Number Legibility Scale

Rating/Description	Example
A/Perfect legibility	0 1 2 3 4 5 6 7 8 9
B/Legible	0 1 2 3 4 5 6 7 8 9
C/Minimum legibility	0 1 2 3 4 5 6 7 8 9
D/Almost illegible	0 1 2 3 4 5 6 7 8 9
E/Illegible	0 1 2 3 4 5 6 7 8 9

NUMERIC KEYPAD

Practice the touch method outside of class by using the replica of a numeric keypad shown below. When loose-leaf page reinforcements are affixed to the key tops, you can feel the simulation of the key tops on an actual calculator. In addition, if the 5 Key on your calculator does not have a raised dot to help locate the home row, you can affix a small piece of self-adhesive paper, such as an address label, to the top of the 5 Key.

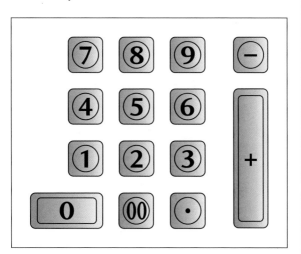

Illus. A-3
Numeric Keypad.

126

Student Data

PERSONAL

Name _____ _____ _____ Date _____
        Last   First   Middle

Address _____ Phone _____

Birth Place _____ Birth Date _____

Father _____ Phone _____

Mother _____ Phone _____

Father's Occupation _____ Workplace _____ Phone _____

Mother's Occupation _____ Workplace _____ Phone _____

EDUCATION

High School _____ School Name _____ City _____ State _____ Years _____

Subject(s): Favorite _____ Least Favorite _____

Specific Career Plan(s) _____

Grade Point Average _____ Math Grade Average _____ English Grade Average _____

What skill, talent, personal trait, etc.:

Is your best? _____

Do you want to develop? _____

INTERESTS

School Activities and/or Honors _____

Outside School Activities _____

COMPUTER EXPERIENCE

Courses and Dates _____

Personal Use _____

Keyboarding: WAM _____ Errors _____

PRESENT EMPLOYMENT

Job Title _____ Company _____

Hours a Week _____ Duties _____

PREVIOUS EMPLOYMENT

Job Titles _____ Companies _____ Dates _____

_____ _____

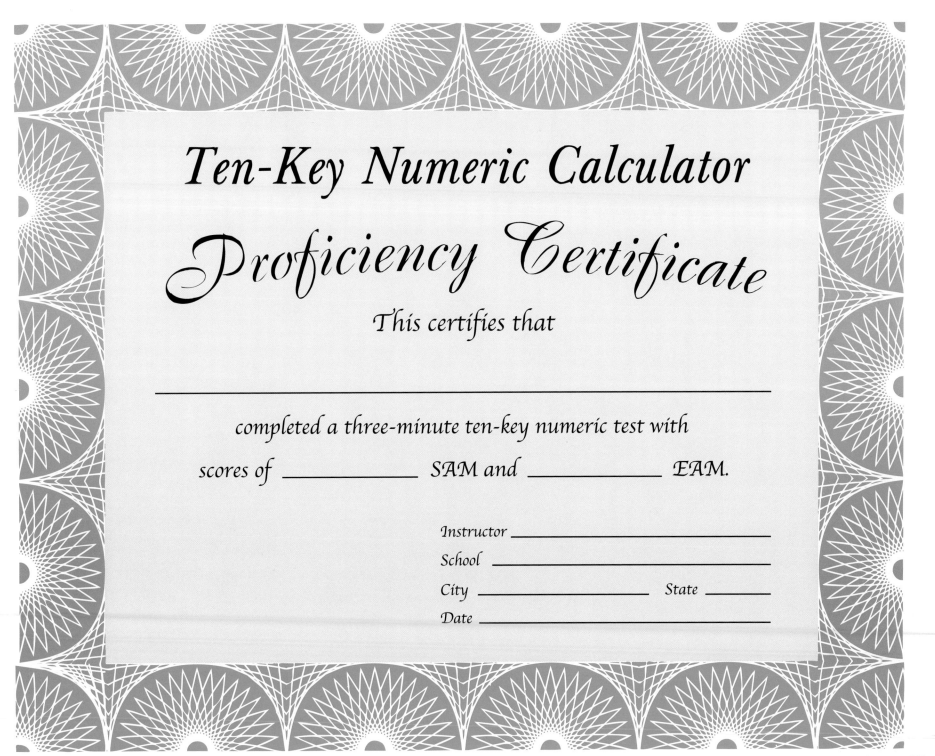

Ten-Key Numeric Calculator

Proficiency Certificate

This certifies that

_____

completed a three-minute ten-key numeric test with

scores of _____ SAM and _____ EAM.

Instructor _____

School _____

City _____ State _____

Date _____

TEN-KEY NUMERIC TEST #1

	(A)	(B)	(C)	(D)	(E)
	342,511	619,395	48,763	428,065	92,173
	65,185	2,355	267,829	2,547	124,569
	1,556	366,011	4,685	65,134	3,215
25 strokes →	216,158	85,396	793,221	193,767	348,975
	4,622	571,322	136,091	54,619	9,146
	713,586	15,622	3,982	327,943	64,188
	438,966	1,534	21,470	8,543	204,925
	7,449	46,088	81,335	68,125	72,516
50 strokes →	1,790,033	1,707,723	1,357,376	1,148,743	919,707

	(F)	(G)	(H)	(I)	(J)
	6,292	734,823	126,424	19,572	412,437
	413,528	6,513	85,451	5,456	35,725
	85,583	87,529	221,986	342,261	2,924
25 strokes →	372,916	193,182	5,562	471,297	885,741
	885,457	64,432	73,582	6,958	55,482
	652,643	876,525	4,198	52,938	83,546
	651	53,267	92,213	15,423	7,552
	85,914	2,475	675,523	756,825	578,818
50 strokes →	2,502,984	2,018,746	1,284,939	1,670,730	2,062,225

	(K)	(L)	(M)	(N)	(O)
	235,478	345,513	45,894	4,587	37,825
	528,748	85,324	155,652	961,483	831,928
	7,566	83,622	723,489	38,621	93,456
25 strokes →	15,725	55,722	2,154	359,418	62,846
	732,249	127,469	8,329	97,487	48,952
	187,562	7,534	145,238	16,423	492,853
	44,587	94,223	86,984	185,531	71,789
	632	36,232	13,752	6,832	1,729
50 strokes →	1,752,547	835,639	1,181,492	1,670,382	1,641,378

Total Strokes ÷ 3 minutes = SAM
Total Errors ÷ 3 minutes = EAM
Record your scores on the TKNTest Record on page 120.

TEN-KEY NUMERIC TEST #2

	(A)	(B)	(C)	(D)	(E)
	542,186	728,295	25,378	519,674	31,593
	76,183	2,263	265,529	2,136	135,506
	2,664	367,932	4,876	64,134	3,522
25 strokes →	225,168	84,936	748,325	182,787	457,711
	4,621	752,323	135,183	54,528	9,766
	713,688	16,861	6,386	417,841	86,209
	329,976	1,244	44,519	8,436	215,923
	5,595	46,919	72,326	79,143	73,686
50 strokes →	1,900,081	2,000,773	1,302,522	1,328,679	1,013,916

	(F)	(G)	(H)	(I)	(J)
	5,281	431,600	226,523	35,628	512,389
	313,609	6,312	97,452	5,438	34,716
	82,563	87,506	213,975	341,161	2,831
25 strokes →	361,926	183,284	5,631	467,196	875,842
	889,346	47,952	82,572	7,429	57,416
	852,543	869,524	4,186	52,847	82,658
	642	53,265	91,113	15,323	7,431
	82,734	6,716	663,523	757,926	588,928
50 strokes →	2,588,644	1,686,159	1,384,975	1,682,948	2,162,211

	(K)	(L)	(M)	(N)	(O)
	743,206	234,614	52,973	5,698	33,251
	519,728	96,464	152,752	972,586	932,329
	4,988	83,723	721,598	32,264	56,692
25 strokes →	14,825	47,722	3,125	446,429	61,546
	731,259	127,569	8,538	96,387	57,251
	185,872	7,545	142,259	15,234	493,965
	43,488	96,225	78,974	195,531	81,742
	357	48,241	15,542	6,452	2,573
50 strokes →	2,243,723	742,103	1,175,761	1,770,581	1,719,349

Total Strokes ÷ 3 minutes = SAM
Total Errors ÷ 3 minutes = EAM
Record your scores on the TKNTest Record on page 120.

Index

Index

Index

Index